FLOYD CLYMER'S MOTORCYCLIST'S LIBRARY

The Book of the
NORTON

A PRACTICAL GUIDE ON THE HANDLING AND MAINTENANCE OF ALL 1938-56 S.V. AND O.H.V. SINGLE-CYLINDER NORTONS EXCEPT TRIALS MODELS

BY

W. C. HAYCRAFT
F.R.S.A.

ANNOUNCEMENT

By special arrangement with the original publishers of this book, Sir Isaac Pitman & Son, Ltd., of London, England, we have secured the exclusive publishing rights for this book, as well as all others in THE MOTORCYCLIST'S LIBRARY.

Included in THE MOTORCYCLIST'S LIBRARY are complete instruction manuals covering the care and operation of respective motorcycles and engines; valuable data on speed tuning, and thrilling accounts of motorcycle race events. See listing of available titles elsewhere in this edition.

We consider it a privilege to be able to offer so many fine titles to our customers.

FLOYD CLYMER
Publisher of Books Pertaining to Automobiles and Motorcycles

2125 W. PICO ST.　　　　　　　　　　LOS ANGELES 6, CALIF.

INTRODUCTION

Welcome to the world of digital publishing ~ the book you now hold in your hand, while unchanged from the original edition, was printed using the latest state of the art digital technology. The advent of print-on-demand has forever changed the publishing process, never has information been so accessible and it is our hope that this book serves your informational needs for years to come. If this is your first exposure to digital publishing, we hope that you are pleased with the results. Many more titles of interest to the classic automobile and motorcycle enthusiast, collector and restorer are available via our website at www.VelocePress.com. We hope that you find this title as interesting as we do.

NOTE FROM THE PUBLISHER

The information presented is true and complete to the best of our knowledge. All recommendations are made without any guarantees on the part of the author or the publisher, who also disclaim all liability incurred with the use of this information.

TRADEMARKS

We recognize that some words, model names and designations, for example, mentioned herein are the property of the trademark holder. We use them for identification purposes only. This is not an official publication.

INFORMATION ON THE USE OF THIS PUBLICATION

This manual is an invaluable resource for the classic motorcycle enthusiast and a "must have" for owners interested in performing their own maintenance. However, in today's information age we are constantly subject to changes in common practice, new technology, availability of improved materials and increased awareness of chemical toxicity. As such, it is advised that the user consult with an experienced professional prior to undertaking any procedure described herein. While every care has been taken to ensure correctness of information, it is obviously not possible to guarantee complete freedom from errors or omissions or to accept liability arising from such errors or omissions. Therefore, any individual that uses the information contained within, or elects to perform or participate in do-it-yourself repairs or modifications acknowledges that there is a risk factor involved and that the publisher or its associates cannot be held responsible for personal injury or property damage resulting from the use of the information or the outcome of such procedures.

WARNING!

One final word of advice, this publication is intended to be used as a reference guide, and when in doubt the reader should consult with a qualified technician.

PREFACE

The author has aimed at providing a *readable* book of reference (for novices and experts), and has spared no pains to make it as complete as possible. He has in preparing the MS. derived a pleasure second only to that which actual Norton riding experience on a Model 18 has given him.

The products of Norton Motors, Ltd., Bracebridge Street, Birmingham, 6 (Phone: Aston Cross 3711) need no introduction. Their stamina, power, reliability, and tenacious road holding are renowned everywhere and have been amply demonstrated by famous riders such as Duke, Amm, Daniell, Woods, Guthrie, and Frith.

The present edition of this handbook contains *all* essential maintenance and stripping-down instructions for the following Nortons—

1. The 1938–54 490 c.c., 596 c.c. S.V. Models 16H, 1.
2. The 1938–54 350 c.c., 490 c.c. O.H.V. Models 50, 55, 18, 20, ES2.
3. The 1955 490 c.c., 596 c.c. O.H.V. Models ES2, 19R, 19S.
4. The 1956 350 c.c., 490 c.c., 596 c.c. O.H.V. Models 50, ES2, 19S.

Note that the 1938–54 S.V. Model 1 is often referred to as the "Big 4." All S.V. Nortons were discontinued after 1954, but Model 19 (an ideal sidecar job) was added to the O.H.V. range in 1955. It was available (Model 19R) with a rigid frame or (Model 19S) with "swinging arm" rear suspension of the type used on Model ES2. For 1956 the rigid frame Model 19R has been dropped, but Model 19S is being continued. A 350 c.c. newcomer is Model 50 which has a specification similar to that of Model ES2. All machines embody worth-while improvements giving more power, less noise, better riding positions, and enhanced appearance.

Instructions not dated in this handbook apply to all 1938 and later models. The following machines are not covered: the O.H.C. (overhead-camshaft), the Trials, and the twin-cylinder models.

I thank Norton Motors, Ltd., for assistance in regard to technical data, and for according me permission to reproduce various Norton copyright illustrations. I am also grateful to some accessory firms for their helpful co-operation. Finally, I wish all Norton owners maximum trouble-free mileage at minimum cost.

W. C. H.

CONTENTS

I. HANDLING A NORTON 1
   Preliminaries—Use of controls

II. THE LIGHTING EQUIPMENT 11
   Dynamo maintenance—Care of the battery—The lamps—Bulb renewal—The lighting switch and horn

III. LUBRICATION 30
   Engine lubrication—The motor-cycle parts

IV. THE AMAL CARBURETTOR 40
   How it works (1938–54)—How it works (1955 onwards)—Tuning the carburettor—Maintenance

V. GENERAL MAINTENANCE 58
   Tools, etc.—The ignition system—Valve clearances—Decarbonizing 1938–47 models—Decarbonizing 1948–56 models—Ignition and valve timing—Engine overhaul—The transmission—Wheels, brakes, and tyres—Steering head, forks, frame, etc.

Index 143

CHAPTER I

HANDLING A NORTON

It is assumed that you have bought a brand new or a second-hand Norton. If you are a complete novice, there are a number of points with which you must become fully conversant before taking to the road. A useful book, especially for beginners, is *The Art of Motor Cycling* (Pitman, 5s.). This

Fig. 1. A Well-proved and Popular O.H.V. "Five Hundred" —the Robust and Powerful Model ES2 Norton with Light-alloy Head and "Swinging Arm" Rear Suspension

The Model ES2 has an engine capacity of 490 c.c., the bore and stroke being 79 mm × 100 mm. Above is shown a 1956 model. The spring-frame Model 50 and the spring-frame Model 19S are similar, but they have an engine capacity of 348 c.c. and 596 c.c., the bore and stroke being 71 mm × 88 mm and 82 × 113 mm respectively.

covers every aspect of riding, legal matters, clothing, accessories, etc. Obtain and read carefully a copy of the latest edition of the *Highway Code*.

The Riding Position. If this is not entirely satisfactory, it is possible to make a combined adjustment of the handlebars, handlebar controls, and footrests. The handlebars (except 1938–9 insulated type) can readily be adjusted after slackening the four securing bolts, and clip fittings enable the positions of the handlebar levers to be varied. The shafts for the footrest hangers and the shaft for the gear-change pedal are serrated and splined respectively, and an appreciable variation in the position of the footrests and pedal is possible.

With the riding position correct, the body should be nicely balanced and poised slightly forwards, with the arms practically straight and the hands gently resting on the handlebar grips. The angle between the thighs and the lower parts of the legs should be very slightly less than a right-angle and the rear of the sole should rest comfortably on each footrest, with the toe in such a position that upward and downward gear changes can be made without moving the foot from the footrest.

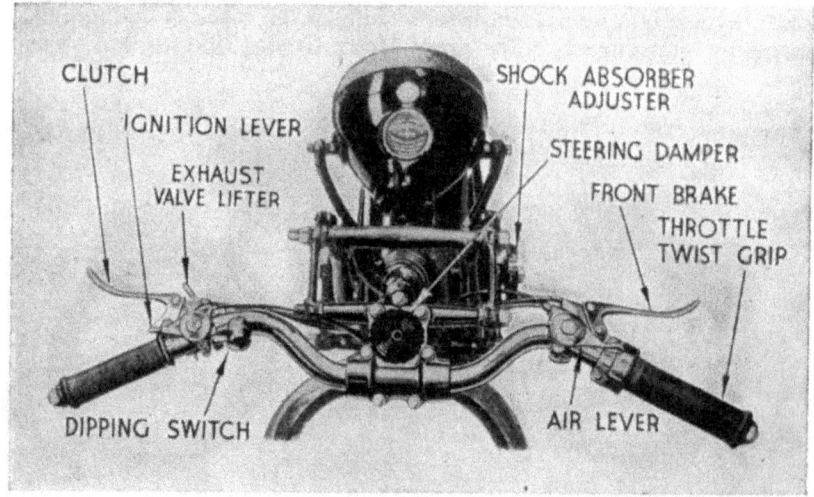

FIG. 2. THE CONTROL LAYOUT (1938–46 MODELS)

USE OF CONTROLS

Layout and Handling. The layout of the controls on 1938–56 S.V. and O.H.V. Nortons is shown in Figs. 2 and 3. Controls fall into two groups: (1) engine controls, and (2) motor-cycle controls. If you are a complete novice, sit on the saddle of your mount, and "twiddle" the various levers while meditating on what the effect would be if the engine were running. Those handling a Norton for the first time should note the following—

1. All handlebar controls (including the throttle twist-grip) are operated by *inward* movement.

2. The throttle twist-grip (which controls engine speed) has a full movement of approximately *one-quarter* of a complete turn. With the throttle-stop correctly set to provide good tick-over, the throttle slide does not close completely. On most Nortons it is essential to use a very small

throttle opening (about one-sixteenth to one-eighth of an inch as measured at the rim of the twist-grip rubber) for starting purposes, otherwise some difficulty may be experienced in making a start. 1946–54 Nortons have an easy-starter screw (*see* page 43).

3. The air lever (which enables the mixture of air and petrol to be varied) must be kept closed completely for starting from *cold* but at all other times it should normally be *wide open*. Slight closing when travelling slowly under load, to ward off a tendency for pinking, may sometimes be desirable, but it is generally best to use the ignition lever to forestall pinking.

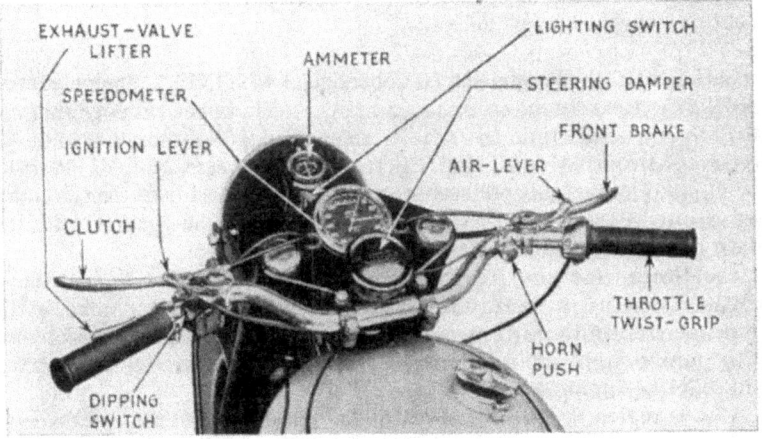

Fig. 3. The Control Layout (1947 Onwards)

The machine shown is a 1955 Model ES2, but the layout is the same on all 1947 and later O.H.V. models. On the 1956 range, however, the instrument panel is omitted, the speedometer, ammeter, and lighting switch being on a panel built into the Lucas pre-focus type headlamp. The horn push is also combined with the dipping switch on the near side of the handlebars.

4. The ignition lever (which moves the contact-breaker base on the magneto portion of the "Magdyno") should always be kept fully, or nearly fully, advanced while riding, except when pinking occurs. Then the ignition should be temporarily retarded a shade, but note that this automatically reduces the power output. At the first opportunity after temporary retardation, the ignition lever should be *advanced as far as possible*. For starting purposes, however, it is always advisable to retard the ignition lever to at least the half-way position.

5. Never use the exhaust-valve lifter (which raises the exhaust valve off its seat) for any purpose other than starting and stopping the engine. It is permissible, however, to use it occasionally when descending hills, provided that the throttle is shut right back and the air lever is wide open.

6. The clutch lever (which disconnects and re-connects the drive from the engine to the rear wheel) must always be used *fully* and *progressively*. Use it only when moving off and during each gear change.

7. The foot gear-change pedal on the off-side of the gearbox provides four gear ratios and "neutral" which lies between first and second gears. Note that "neutral" should only be obtained *after* engaging first gear. All downward changes (*see* Fig. 5) are made by upward movement of the pedal with the toe, and all upward changes are made by downward movement of the pedal with the toe. The gear-change pedal returns to the same (horizontal) position after each gear change is effected, ready for the next change to be made. During each gear change it is necessary to make a *full* movement of the gear-change pedal.

Fuel and Oil Replenishment. It is beneficial with O.H.V. engines, especially during the running-in period, to add a little upper-cylinder lubricant to the petrol each time the tank is replenished. Suitable lubricants are Redex, Castrollo, Mixtrol, B.P. Energol UCL, Filtrate Colloidal Petroyle, etc. Liquid lubricant is preferable to that in tablet form, and the container cap is often employed as a measure. Alternatively the garage hand will inject one or two "shots" after tanking up with petrol.

The Norton fuel tank (capacity: $2\frac{3}{4}$ gal; 1956 models, $3\frac{1}{4}$ gal) has at its base a decent-size gauze filter, but never neglect to use a funnel with a filter when replenishing from a can, as impurities are apt to form a sediment at the tank bottom and interfere with free supply to the engine, due to the tank filter becoming clogged.

Always replenish the oil tank with the correct brand and grade of oil recommended by Norton Motors, Ltd. (*see* Chapter III). Before checking the oil level, run the engine a few minutes to scavenge the sump. The oil level in the tank should not be above approximately 2 in. from the top of the filler cap (or the tank more than three-quarters full on 1946–56 models), and should never be allowed to fall below the half-full level in the tank (*see* page 33).

If the oil level is below the half-full mark (the minimum oil level is marked on the outside of the tank), the insufficient oil in circulation tends to overheat. If the tank is topped up too high, pressure built up inside the tank by the oil return pipe will force surplus oil through the air-release pipe on to the road.

Norton Motors, Ltd., recommend the addition of some running-in compound (containing "colloidal graphite") to the *engine oil* during the running-in period. The usual proportions to use are *one pint* of running-in compound to each gallon of oil, but if use of the compound is continued after running-in, the quantity added should be halved.

Always Maintain Correct Tyre Pressures. The pressures should be checked weekly. Suitable pressure gauges are the Dunlop No. 6, Holdtite,

HANDLING A NORTON

Romac, and Schrader No. 7750. To use a gauge, the valve dust cap (Fig. 4) is taken off, and the end of the pressure gauge is pressed on to the open end of the valve. It depresses the pin and allows air to enter the gauge and push up the piston calibrated in pounds per square inch. Always keep the dust caps screwed on firmly! Dust or grit getting into the valve stem is liable to interfere with the valve action of the little spring-controlled plunger (Fig. 4) and cause leakage. About once a year valve "insides" should be replaced. They can be removed by taking off the valve cap and using the slotted end as a screwdriver.

Correct solo pressures for 26 in. × 3·25 in. (3·25–19) tyres are 20 lb per sq in. for the front tyre and 23 lb per sq in. for the rear tyre, where

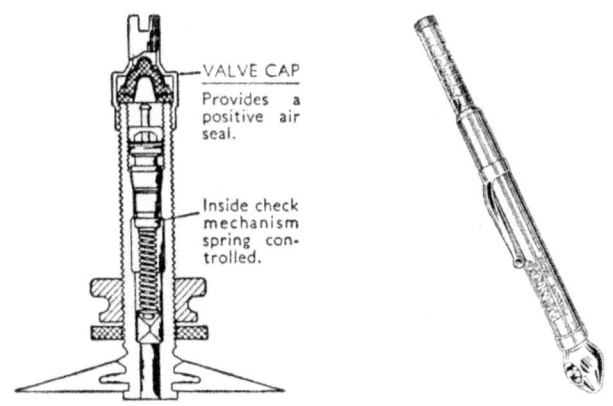

FIG. 4. SHOWING (LEFT) DUNLOP VALVE AND (RIGHT) DUNLOP NO. 6 POCKET PRESSURE GAUGE

telescopic front forks are fitted. On machines with girder-type front forks, inflate front and rear tyres to the above pressures. Where a pillion passenger is carried, add 2–3 lb per sq in. to the pressure of the rear tyre. Note that Models 19R and 19S have a 26 in. × 4·00 in. (4·00–18) rear tyre and the correct normal tyre pressure is 24 lb per sq in. (solo) and 25 lb per sq in. (sidecar) for the rear tyre. Where a sidecar is fitted to Model 19R or 19S the correct normal pressure for the front tyre is 22 lb per sq in. instead of 20 lb per sq in. If heavy luggage is carried it is desirable to take this into account and increase the pressure of the rear tyre by several lb per sq in.

Setting Controls for Starting Up (1938 Onwards). First make sure that there is sufficient oil of the correct grade in the oil tank, gearbox, and oil-bath chain case (*see* Chapter III), and that the various motor-cycle parts have been properly lubricated. The oil tank holds four pints (*see* page 4). Also check that the tyre pressures are correct (*see* previous paragraph), and that there is sufficient petrol in the tank which holds 2¾ gal (1956 models, 3¼ gal). Pull your Norton backward on to its rear or spring-up centre stand and prepare to start up. Note that when attempting to start up with the machine off its stand, it is advisable to stand astride the machine, as this helps to balance it. On a Norton with a reserve petrol tap, verify that the reserve tap (the off-side one) is turned off, and turn on the main tap. To turn on a tap, press the hexagonal button; to turn off, press the knurled button. There is no oil tap provided.

To obtain a quick start, it is important to set the controls correctly. Verify that the foot gear-change pedal is in the "neutral" position, i.e. between first and second gears (*see* Fig. 5). Make sure that movement of the kick-starter pedal does not rotate the rear wheel, with the clutch engaged. On 1938–45 and 1955 and later Nortons open the throttle very slightly by turning the twist-grip *inwards* about one-eighth of an inch (as measured at the rim of the twist-grip rubber). On 1946–54 models do not open the throttle twist-grip prior to starting up. Instead, turn the tommy-bar of the easy-starter screw (*see* Fig. 29) as far as possible *clockwise*, so as to raise the throttle slide to the best position for starting.

If the engine is stone cold, close the air lever completely, and retard the ignition lever so that it is half-way between the full advance and full retard positions. Also momentarily depress the tickler on the float chamber, but do not flood the carburettor so that petrol begins to drip. If the engine has been previously warmed up, the air lever should be opened one-third approximately (less for engines with "monobloc" carburettor), and the carburettor tickler should not be touched. It is assumed there is no back-lash in the controls.

Difficult engine starting is often attributable to faulty control setting, and it is essential to *keep the throttle lever nearly closed* when endeavouring to start. Only thus can a high velocity air stream be induced over the pilot jet. 1946–54 models have an easy-starting screw (*see* page 51) and the twist-grip is completely closed for starting.

Starting Up. If the engine is unduly stiff in cold weather, free the piston before attempting to start up. The best method is to kick the engine over quickly about half a dozen times, with the exhaust-valve lifter fully raised.

To start, stand astride or beside the machine, put the piston on compression, raise the exhaust-valve lifter and depress the kick-starter a further 2–3 in. Release the exhaust valve lifter and permit the kick-starter to return to its normal position. Then give a long swinging kick, carrying the starter round as far as possible. With the engine and carburettor in proper order, a start should be effected on the third kick at the most. Failure to start quickly is usually due to some definite defect such as plug trouble (*see* page 63).

A prevalent source of difficult engine-starting is an over-rich mixture caused by excessive flooding of the carburettor or by numerous ineffectual attempts with the kick-starter, made worse perhaps by a low temperature.

To clear the combustion chamber of vaporized fuel, open both the throttle twist-grip and air lever to their full extent and kick over the engine several times.

When the engine starts up, turn the easy-starter screw (1946–54) *anti-clockwise* to its normal position, and adjust the controls to give a sweet "pilot" tick-over. Advance the air lever fully, or nearly fully, and similarly advance the ignition lever. Do not "rev" up the engine *until the oil is circulating properly and has warmed up*. Sudden engine racing, especially when not under load, is most injurious. Never continue to run an engine in a closed garage, and do not allow a cold engine to run too slowly; this causes low-temperature condensation. If a dry-sump lubricated engine starts to issue clouds of blue smoke when starting up, ignore this phenomenon, as the surplus oil will quickly be returned to the tank by the pump. Black smoke denotes an over-rich mixture. Instructions for tuning the carburettor will be found on page 47.

Check Oil Circulation After Starting Up. Remove the oil filler cap and observe the oil issuing from the return pipe. After the engine has run a few minutes (*see* page 34) the return is spasmodic.

To Engage First Gear. Disengage the clutch by squeezing the handlebar lever, and move the foot gear-change pedal *upwards* to its *full* extent. If you fail to engage first gear readily with the motor-cycle stationary, rock the machine gently to and from while maintaining slight pressure on the foot gear-change pedal (Fig. 5). Continue doing this until you feel that first gear is engaged.

Moving Off. Open the throttle slightly by turning the throttle twist-grip *inwards*, and gently and progressively engage the clutch by releasing the handlebar lever. As the clutch engages and the motor-cycle gathers momentum, open the throttle a little more. Should any slight pinking occur, immediately retard the ignition very slightly, or close the air lever a shade. For all normal running after the engine has warmed up, keep the ignition lever fully advanced and the air lever wide open.

Change from First to Second Gear. Gear-changing is rapidly mastered, and gear crashing of a serious nature is impossible because all pinions are of the constant-mesh type. Speed up the machine to about 15 m.p.h., declutch, and simultaneously throttle down the engine, wait a second until mainshaft and layshaft are running at the same speed, and depress the foot change fully, afterwards letting in the clutch gently and throttling up to take the increased load. *Never employ force on the foot change.* All operations should be quick, but accurate and progressive, and *no attempt should ever be made to change gear without first declutching,* for in this case we have dog clutches being induced to mesh while being driven at different speeds. *On no account allow the engine to knock* (i.e. make a metallic noise) by driving it too slowly under load or with too advanced ignition timing. A change to a lower gear should be made immediately the engine shows signs of distress, *but do not slip the clutch as an alternative to gear-changing*.

Change from Second to Third Gear. Proceed as before. Speed up the machine until it has plenty of momentum, declutch, throttle down, wait a second, and smartly move the foot change down fully until third gear is felt to engage; afterwards engage the clutch and throttle up again until the desired speed is reached.

Change from Third to Fourth Gear. To get into top gear, follow the previous procedure. Throttle up, declutch, ease off the throttle, wait momentarily and push the pedal down until fourth gear is felt to engage.

The tendency for knocking, if any, is during the change from third to fourth, and the controls should be handled judiciously to counteract this, especially if the change is made on an up-gradient, when the engine revolutions should be kept high during the changes.

Making Downward Gear Changes. Simultaneously open the throttle slightly, disengage the clutch, and with toe pressure *raise* the foot gear-change pedal upwards to its full extent. Then quickly and progressively re-engage the clutch.

When making a gear change, hold the foot gear-change pedal in position with the toe until the gear is *felt* to engage and the clutch has been re-engaged. Make all gear changes quietly and smoothly.

Note that when changing down quickly from fourth or third gear into first gear it is not essential to disengage the clutch, to throttle up the engine, and to *re-engage the clutch* during each gear change. It is sufficient to slow down to a low speed, disengage the clutch, and make two or three full upward movements of the gear-change pedal in quick succession, according to whether third or fourth gear respectively was previously engaged. Each time you raise the gear-change pedal, "blip" the engine, i.e. throttle up slightly.

To Obtain "Neutral." It is necessary to change down into first gear, stop,* and then with the clutch still disengaged, *slightly* and very gently *depress* the foot gear-change pedal with the toe. In this instance do not move the pedal to its full extent, otherwise you will miss "neutral" and engage second gear. A "light touch" is required, and you should be careful to re-engage the clutch gradually in case a gear should have been accidentally engaged. Neutral lies between first and second gears (*see* Fig. 5).

* An expert can obtain neutral without first stopping the machine.

Running-in. After taking delivery of a brand new Norton, certain care must be exercised for a period when driving. *Until 500 miles have been covered, a speed in excess of 35 m.p.h. in top gear should not be attained;* keep down to correspondingly lower maximum speeds in the other gears, and nurse a new or rebored engine carefully for 1,000 miles. Besides avoiding excessive speed, avoid opening the throttle more than one-quarter to one-third, and never allow the engine to labour, otherwise it will never

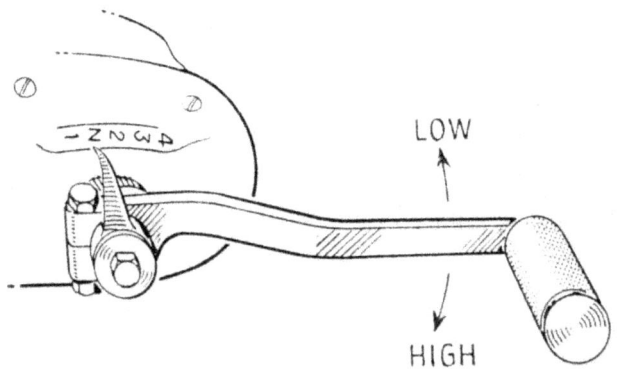

FIG. 5. THE FOOT GEAR-CHANGE PEDAL AND INDICATOR
The pedal automatically returns to the same position after each gear change.

attain maximum efficiency, and its performance will probably be spoiled (*see also* page 33).

Piston Seizure. Piston seizure is the only kind of seizure likely to arise through over-driving a new machine which has not been thoroughly run-in. If piston seizure (indicated by sudden loss of power and gradual slowing up) should occur, whip out the clutch and throttle down instantly. Allow the engine to cool before continuing, and at the first opportunity examine the cylinder barrel and piston for scoring. Slight scoring of the piston skirt can sometimes be overlooked, and the same applies to very slight score marks on the cylinder bore. But if the cylinder bore is marred by numerous and rather deep scores, it will be necessary to have the cylinder barrel rebored and an oversize piston and rings fitted. Pre-ignition, due to an unsuitable plug, produces symptoms rather similar to those of piston seizure.

Suitable Lodge and K.L.G. Plugs. On the S.V. Model 16H (up to 1947) and on Model 1—the Big 4—(up to 1949), requiring 18 mm plugs, fit a Lodge H3 or H1 respectively, or else a K.L.G. type M80. The H1 and the M80 are suitable for Model 19 (up to 1940). On O.H.V. models (pre-1956) requiring 14 mm plugs suitable types are the Lodge HLN and the K.L.G. FE70 or F70 (pre-1955 Models 18, ES2). On 1948-54 S.V. models (16H and Big Four) requiring 14 mm plugs, it is advisable to fit the Lodge HLN or the K.L.G. FE70. Watertight plugs and terminal covers are also available, as well as "ignition-supression" type plugs and terminal covers (compulsory on machines registered for the first time after 1st July 1953). The reader is also referred to the back of the dust cover.

Note that for the 1956 (high compression) O.H.V. engines Norton Motors, Ltd., recommend the fitting of a 14 mm Lodge 2HLN or a K.L.G. FE80.

Champion Plugs. On early S.V. engines requiring 18 mm plugs, fit a type 16 Champion. On all later S.V. models requiring 14 mm plugs, use a Champion NA-8. On all O.H.V. models (taking 14 mm plugs), also fit a Champion NA-8. Note that Champion plugs are of the non-detachable type and cannot be dismantled for cleaning (*see* page 66).

CHAPTER II

THE LIGHTING EQUIPMENT

INSTRUCTIONS for the maintenance of the magneto unit of the "Magdyno" are on page 66. This chapter deals with the dynamo portion alone, together with the lamps and battery. The following instructions apply from 1938 onwards (*see also* page 35).

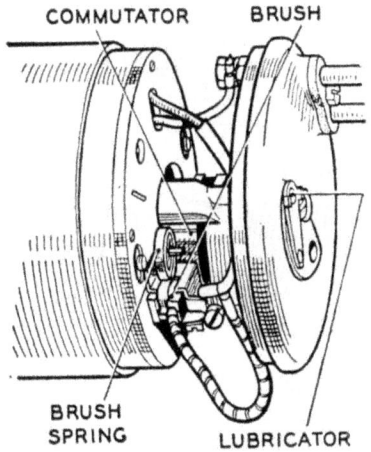

FIG. 6. COMMUTATOR END OF LUCAS E3HM DYNAMO
Some thin machine oil should be put in the lubricator about every 3,000 miles.
Later Nortons have the E3LM dynamo (Fig. 6A).

DYNAMO MAINTENANCE

Before interfering with the wiring, always disconnect the battery positive lead (about one foot long)* from the switch lead, to avoid the danger of short circuits which might cause serious damage. To disconnect, move the rubber shield and unscrew the cable connector; do not touch the frame with the connector and cause a short circuit. When reconnecting, pull the rubber shield well over the connector.

* On 1953 and later Nortons having a "pre-focus" type headlamp, a positive-earth system is used, and the battery *negative* lead should be disconnected.

If at any time the motor-cycle must be ridden with the battery disconnected, or in any way out of service, it is essential to run with the switch in the "OFF" position (compensated-voltage-control excepted).

Inspection of Brushgear. It is advisable about every six months to remove the metal cover-band from the dynamo and inspect the brushgear and commutator. When removing the cover-band it is not necessary to disconnect either lead from the battery.

See that the dynamo brushes work freely in their holders. This can be easily ascertained by holding back each retaining spring and gently pulling

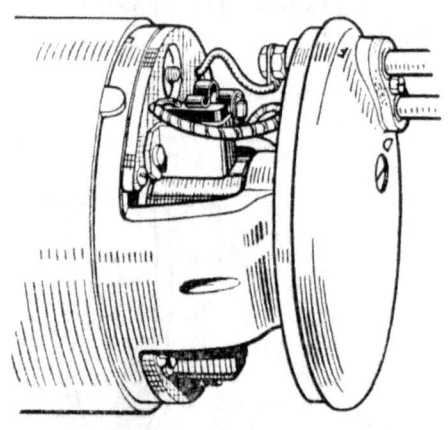

FIG. 6A. COMMUTATOR END OF LUCAS E3LM DYNAMO
No lubricator is fitted.

each flexible lead; the brush should move without the slightest sluggishness. It should also return to its original position directly the lead is let go. When testing a brush in this way, release it gently, otherwise it may get chipped. The brushes should be clean and "bed" over the whole surface; that is, the face in contact with the commutator should appear uniformly polished. Dirty or sticking brushes may be cleaned, after removal, with a cloth moistened with petrol. Always replace carbon brushes in their original positions and see that they make firm contact with the commutator segments.

If the brushes become badly worn, remove them as follows. Release the eyelet on the brush lead by unscrewing the hexagonal nut or screw at the terminal. Then, holding back the spring lever out of the way, withdraw the brush from its holder. Replace with genuine Lucas brushes.

The brush springs should be inspected occasionally to see that they have sufficient tension to keep the brushes firmly pressed against the commutator

THE LIGHTING EQUIPMENT   13

when the machine is running; keep this in mind when the brushes have been in use a long time and are very much worn down. It is unwise to insert brushes of a grade other than that supplied with the dynamo, or to change the tension springs. When the brushes become so worn that they no longer bed down on the commutator, go to a Lucas service agent.

Commutator. The surface of the commutator should be kept clean and free from oil or brush dust, etc. Should any grease or oil work its way on to the commutator through over-lubrication, it will cause sparking and

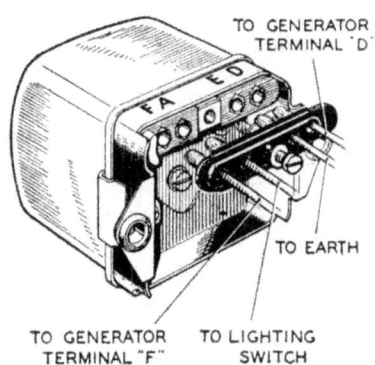

FIG. 7. LUCAS CUT-OUT AND REGULATOR UNIT
SHOWING THE CONNEXIONS

On earlier models the connexions are in the sequence F, A, D, E and two
screws are used to hold the clamping plate.

carbon and copper dust will be collected in the grooves between the commutator segments. The best way to clean the commutator without disconnecting any leads is to remove from its holder one of the two brushes and, inserting a dry duster in the holder, hold it, with a suitably-shaped piece of wood, against the commutator surface, causing the armature to be rotated at the same time. If the commutator has been neglected for a long period, it may need cleaning with fine glasspaper. The segments should be *dark bronze* and highly polished.

Terminals. On a Lucas "Magdyno" with a separate voltage-control unit the positive dynamo terminal is marked D and the shunt-field terminal F on the cover. To connect, first slacken the fixing screws on the terminal block and remove the clamping plate. Then withdraw the metal sleeve from each terminal. The cables should then be passed through the clamping plate holes and bared at the ends for $\frac{3}{8}$ in. Now fit the sleeves over the cables, bend back the wires over them and push the sleeves home into the terminals, finally screwing down the clamping plate shown in Fig. 7.

Lucas Servicing. It is a good plan every 10,000 miles to entrust the dynamo to a Lucas service depot for dismantling, cleaning, servicing, and lubrication.

Compensated Voltage Control. This is used on all 1938 and later Nortons. Wiring diagrams are given on pages 27–29. The control unit comprises the cut-out and voltage control (working on the trembler principle) neatly housed in a casing inside the tool box on all recent Nortons having "swinging arm" rear suspension. On other models it is mounted on the rear mudguard beneath the saddle. The unit sees to it that the battery is kept properly charged automatically, the dynamo output varying according to the state of charge of the battery and the load.

With C.V.C. equipment the lighting switch is provided with only three positions—*Off*, *L*, and *H* (*see* page 22). In all three positions the dynamo gives a controlled output, thus relieving the rider of much responsibility. The regulator begins to operate when the dynamo voltage reaches about 7·3 volts. During daylight running when the battery is well charged the ammeter may indicate a charge of only 1 or 2 amp, for the dynamo gives only a trickle charge. The cut-out prevents the battery discharging when the dynamo is not charging.

The regulator provides for an increase of dynamo output as soon as the lamps are switched on. The effect of switching the lamps on after a long run with the battery voltage high is often to cause a temporary discharge reading at the ammeter, but fairly soon the voltage falls and the regulator responds, thereby causing the output of the dynamo to balance the load of the lamps.

When the battery is in a discharged state, the regulator increases the dynamo output and restores the battery to it normal state of charge in the shortest possible time.

Do Not Tamper with the C.V.C. Unit. The unit is sealed by the makers, and does not need adjustment once it is correctly set. The only conceivable trouble is from the contacts oxidizing or welding together, owing to accidental crossing of the dynamo field and positive leads. Be careful if making wiring alterations (*see* page 11). Referring to Fig. 7, make sure that the C.V.C. unit connexions are correct, tight, and that the insulation is sound.

Removing and Replacing Dynamo. On 1938 and later "Magdyno" models with compensated-voltage-control, first disconnect the connexions from the dynamo terminals. Unscrew the hexagon nut from the "Magdyno" driving-end cover. Then loosen the two screws which fasten the band clip. The dynamo can then be withdrawn from the rest of the "Magdyno" unit.

THE LIGHTING EQUIPMENT

On assembling the dynamo, slide it through the band clip so that the fixing screw passes through the hole in the end cover. See that the gears mesh properly. Tighten the end-cover nut and the two band-clip securing screws. Then connect up the connexions to the dynamo terminals. Verify that this is correctly done. Referring to Fig. 7, it will be noted that the cable from the cut-out and regulator terminal D is connected to a similarly marked terminal on the dynamo. The same applies to the cut-out and regulator terminal marked F.

Absence of Fuses. In order to simplify the system as far as possible, no fuse is provided. If all the connexions are kept clean and tight, there is no possibility of any excess current causing damage to the equipment.

Ammeter. This indicates the amount of current flowing into or from the battery and shows whether the battery is being charged or discharged. It is of the centre-zero type.

CARE OF THE BATTERY

The Lucas battery must receive regular attention to keep it in good condition.

The following are the most important maintenance hints—
1. Keep the electrolyte level with the tops of the separators.
2. Add only distilled water, never tap water.
3. Test the condition of the battery by taking occasional readings of the specific gravity of the acid with a hydrometer.
4. Never leave the battery in a discharged condition.

Top-up the Cells Monthly. Examine the acid level monthly, and even more frequently in tropical climates. Unscrew and remove the battery clamping screw and washer securing the metal strap on 1938–55 models. On 1956 models the battery is held inside the front compartment of the tool box by a "U" bolt pointing upwards at an angle from the bottom inside corner of the tool-box compartment, and a clamping strap bears on the corner of the battery which has no lid; release the strap. Take off the battery lid (1938–55 models) and remove the three vent plugs. Inspect the hole in each vent plug and make certain that it is not obstructed. A choked vent plug hole will result in an increase of pressure in the cell owing to "gassing," and this may cause trouble. Remove any dirt with a bent wire.

Wipe the top of the battery clean with a rag and verify that the rubber washer, fitted beneath each vent plug to prevent leakage, is in position. After wiping the top of the battery, destroy the rag. See that a supply of clean distilled water is to hand.

Be careful not to hold a naked light near the vents. If the level is below

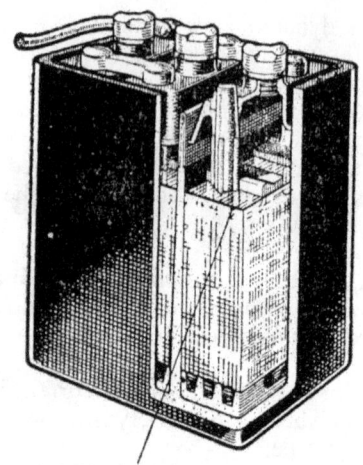

ELECTROLYTE LEVEL

Fig. 8. Keep the Electrolyte Level with the Tops of the Lucas Plate-Separators

On 1956 models the battery is housed with the C.V.C. unit inside the tool box.

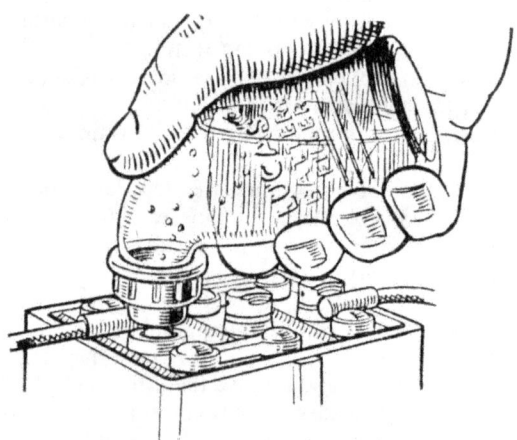

Fig. 9. Topping-up the Cells with a Lucas Battery Filler

Some Lucas batteries (e.g. type PU7E/9) have an acid-level device resting on a ledge below each vent plug orifice. To top-up, pour distilled water round each perforated flange until no more drains into the battery cell.

THE LIGHTING EQUIPMENT

the tops of the separators, add *distilled* water* as required with a Lucas battery filler (*see* Fig. 9) to bring the level correct (*see* Fig. 8). This should be done just *before* a charge run, as the agitation due to running and the gassing will thoroughly mix the solution. Insert the nozzle of the battery filler into each cell until the nozzle rests on the separators. Hold the filler in this position until air bubbles stop rising in the glass container. The cell is then topped-up to the correct level (indicated in Fig. 8).

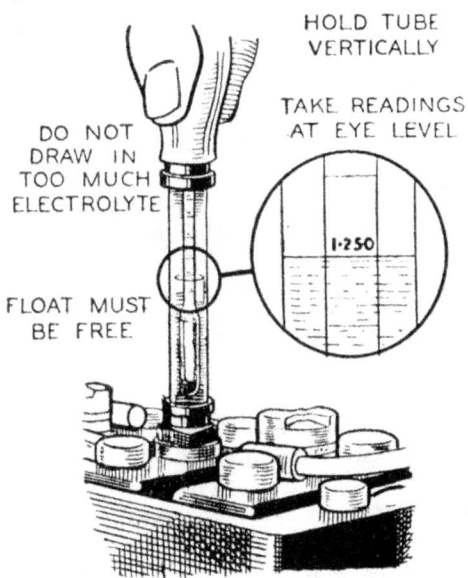

FIG. 10. LUCAS HYDROMETER BEING USED TO CHECK SPECIFIC GRAVITY OF ELECTROLYTE

Acid must not be added to the electrolyte unless the solution has been spilled. If the solution has been spilled by accident, add diluted sulphuric acid of specific gravity equal to that in the cells.

Replenishing the Lucas Battery Filler. When replenishing the Lucas battery filler with distilled water, see that the screw-on nozzle is replaced correctly. The rubber washer must be fitted over the valve with the small peg in the centre of the valve engaging the hole in the projecting boss of the washer.

Checking Specific Gravity. Occasionally, hydrometer readings (specific gravity values) should be taken of the solution in each of the cells. The

* The distilled water, unlike the sulphuric acid, is lost gradually by evaporation.

method of doing this is shown in Fig. 10. The Lucas hydrometer contains a graduated float which indicates the specific gravity of the electrolyte in the battery cell from which a sample is taken.

After a sample has been taken and checked, it must, of course, be returned to the cell. The taking of S.G. readings with a hydrometer is the most efficient way of ascertaining the state of charge of the battery. The S.G. readings should be approximately the *same for all three cells*. Should the reading for one cell differ substantially from the readings for the others, probably some acid has been spilled, or has leaked from the cell concerned. There is also a possibility of a short-circuit between the battery plates. If so, return the battery to a Lucas service depot for attention.

The battery must never be permitted to remain in a discharged condition for long, or serious deterioration will occur. After checking the S.G. readings and topping-up the cells, wipe the top of the battery and remove any spilled electrolyte or water; replace the three vent plugs and the battery lid (pre-1956). Then position and tighten the battery strap.

Battery Connexions. Always keep the connexions clean, free from corrosion, and tight, otherwise the ammeter readings will *not* indicate the true state of charge of the battery. To prevent corrosion, smear screw-type connexions with petroleum jelly.

Correct Readings. With Lucas batteries fitted to Nortons, the specific gravity readings at an acid temperature of approximately 60°F should be: 1·280–1·300, battery fully charged; about 1·200 battery about half discharged; below 1·150, battery fully discharged.

A low state of charge is often caused through parking the machine for long periods with the lighting switch in the *L* position, unaccompanied by much daylight running. The remedy is, of course, to undertake more daylight running and to keep the switch in the *Off* position as much as possible until the battery regains its normal state of charge. If overcharging occurs, have the setting of the compensated-voltage-control unit checked.

Storage. If the equipment is laid by for several months, the battery must be given a small charge from a separate source of electrical energy about once a fortnight, to obviate any permanent sulphation of the plates. In no circumstances must the electrolyte be removed from the battery and the plates allowed to dry, or permanent loss of capacity will result.

THE LAMPS

Several different types of Lucas headlamps and tail lamps have been fitted to 1938 and later Nortons.

The DU142 Headlamp (Pre-1947). This lamp, used on Nortons where no instrument panel is provided, has a double-filament main bulb, one

THE LIGHTING EQUIPMENT 19

filament providing the normal driving light, and the other a dipped beam. The change-over from the normal driving light to the dipped beam is made by a handlebar switch. A small pilot bulb is provided for parking or when driving in town.

An ammeter is incorporated in the lamp. When the lamp is switched on, the ammeter is illuminated by indirect lighting.

To get at the bulbs, release the front fixing clip (*see* Fig. 11) which secures the base of the lamp front and pull the latter outwards. As the

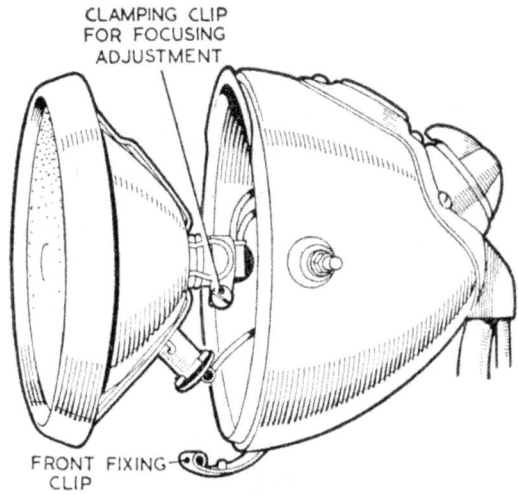

FIG. 11. LUCAS DU142 TYPE HEADLAMP (MANY PRE-1947 MODELS)

lamp front and reflector come away together, free the top tag of the lamp front from the lamp body by lifting the lamp front slightly upwards. When replacing the lamp front and reflector, first locate the top tag in the slot of the lamp body. Afterwards secure the lamp front by means of the front fixing clip.

The D142 Headlamp (Pre-1947). This lamp is used on Nortons with an instrument panel and is very similar to the DU142 headlamp, but it contains neither switch nor ammeter, these being on the tank instrument panel. As with the DU142 headlamp, a double filament main bulb is used, one filament (for normal driving light) being placed at the focus of the reflector, and the other (for dipped beam) being situated slightly above it. A small pilot bulb is also incorporated for parking purposes and when driving in well-illuminated streets. The panel switch positions are the same.

MU42 Headlamp (1947–9). To gain access to the lamp bulbs, release the spring catch at the bottom of the lamp, when the front can be removed.

The reflector is secured to the lamp body by means of a rubber bead, and can be withdrawn when the rubber is removed (*see* Fig. 12.) When refitting, locate the thinner lip of the rubber bead between the reflector rim and the edge of the lamp body. To replace the front, locate the metal

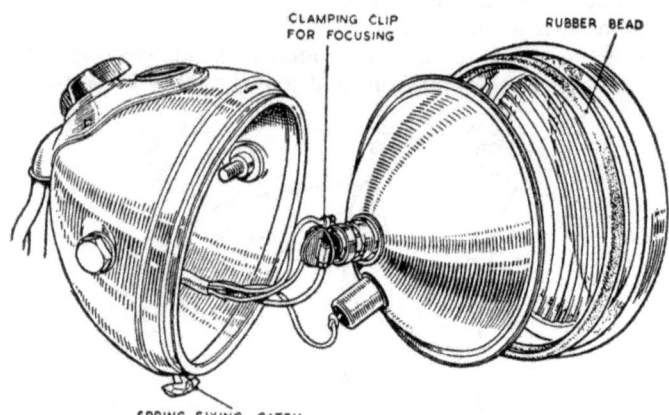

Fig. 12. Lucas MU42 Headlamp with Front and Reflector Removed (1947–9 Models)

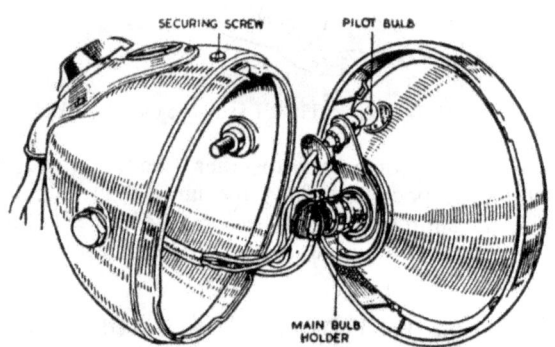

Fig. 13. Lucas SSU700P Headlamp with Front and Light-unit Assembly Removed (1950–2 Models)

tongue in the slot at the top of the lamp, press the front on, and secure with the spring fixing catch.

SSU700P Headlamps (1950–5). To render the bulbs accessible, first remove the lamp front with Lucas light-unit assembly. Slacken the securing screw at the top of the lamp and then detach the front rim, complete with light-unit assembly. When replacing, locate the bottom of the light-unit assembly in the lamp body, press on the front, and secure in position by tightening the securing screw.

The "pre-focus" Lucas SSU700P/1 headlamp with underslung pilot light (Fig. 14) used on all 1953-5 Norton models has *no focusing adjustment*, and the main bulb cannot be inserted incorrectly (*see* page 25). The pilot bulb is carried in a detachable plate.

MCH58 Headlamp (1956). As may be seen in Fig. 15, the speedometer, lighting switch, and ammeter are mounted on a panel secured by three

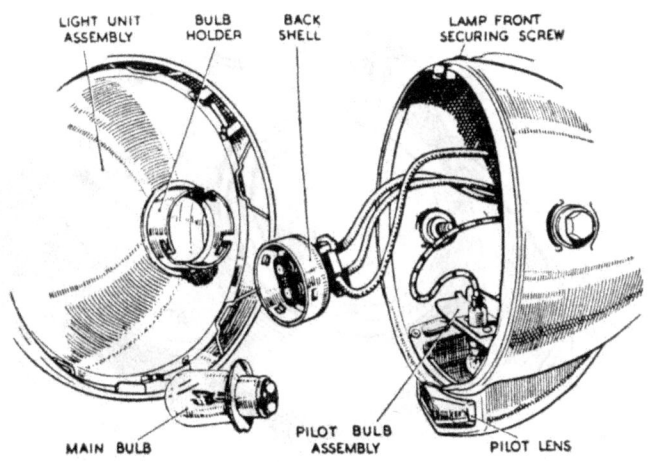

FIG. 14. LUCAS SSU700P/1 "PRE-FOCUS" HEADLAMP WITH LIGHT-UNIT ASSEMBLY (AND MAIN BULB) REMOVED (1953-5 MODELS WITH UNDERSLUNG PILOT LIGHT)

screws to the top of the MCH58 headlamp fitted to all 1956 Nortons. The wiring harness enters through the rear of the lamp body, and is clamped to prevent chafing. The headlamp has a Lucas F700 light-unit assembly which includes a block-type lens and an aluminized reflector, proof against tarnishing.

A plug-in type pilot light (recommended for parking only) is located inside the reflector below the double-filament "pre-focus" main bulb. To gain access to both bulbs, remove the lamp front with sealed-beam light unit assembly, after slackening the securing screw at the top of the lamp. When replacing, locate the bottom of the light unit assembly in the lamp body, press on the front, and secure by tightening the fixing screw at the top of the lamp.

The "pre-focus" main bulb is of the same type (see Fig. 14) as that used

22   THE BOOK OF THE NORTON

with the SSU700P/1 headlamp. It cannot be fitted incorrectly, neither can it be focused.

Switch Positions (1938 Onwards). Compensated-voltage-control is provided on all 1938 and later models, and therefore the dynamo charges the battery when the engine is running with the lighting switch in *any* of its three positions which are as follows—

Off: Headlamp, tail lamp, and sidecar lamp (when fitted) switched off.

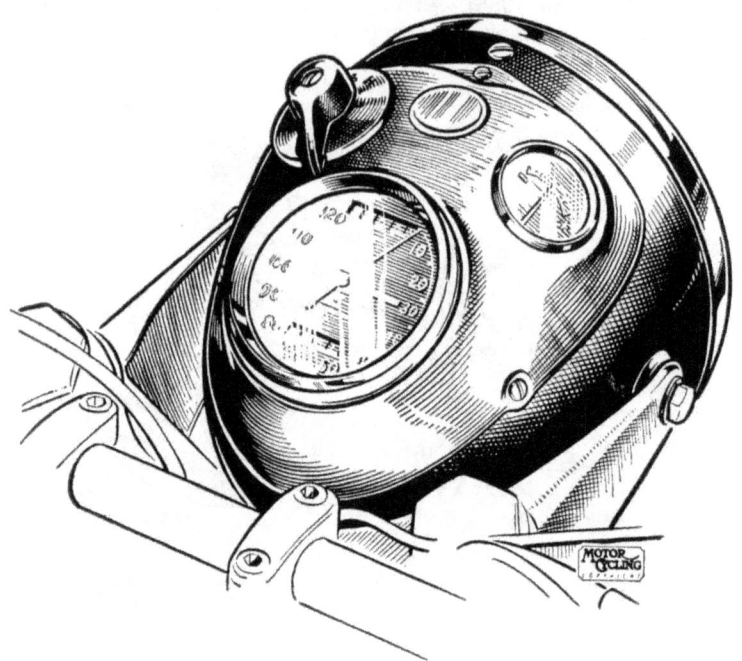

Fig. 15. Lucas MCH58 "Pre-focus" Headlamp with F700 Light-unit Assembly and Panel Housing Speedometer, Ammeter, and Lighting Switch (1956 Models)

(*By courtesy of "Motor Cycling"*)

L: Headlamp pilot bulb, tail lamp, speedometer, and sidecar lamp (where fitted) on.

H: Headlamp main bulb, tail lamp, speedometer, and sidecar lamp (where fitted) on.

Adjusting the Headlamp Position. If the headlamp is incorrectly aligned and/or the main bulb is out of focus, maximum road illumination will not

THE LIGHTING EQUIPMENT

be obtained, and other road users may be inconvenienced by dazzle. It is easy to rectify both faults.

The best method of checking the alignment of the headlamp is to stand your Norton facing a light-coloured wall at a distance of 25–30 feet. Switch on the main driving light and note if the beam is projected straight ahead and parallel with the ground (which should be level).

Take vertical measurements from the centre of the headlamp, and from the centre of the illuminated circle on the wall, to the ground. Both measurements should be equal. If not, loosen the two fixing bolts securing the headlamp in the front fork mounting brackets and tilt the headlamp until the centre of the beam is truly parallel with the ground. Afterwards tighten the two fixing bolts firmly.

Correct Focusing. On all new Nortons the double-filament main bulb is carefully focused to give the best illumination. If Lucas bulbs of the correct wattage and number are fitted as replacements, subsequent re-focusing should not be necessary, unless the focusing adjustment has been disturbed. 1953–5 and 1956 models have the Lucas SSU700P/1 and MCH58 headlamps respectively; these have a main bulb which is permanently "pre-focused" and non-adjustable.

Narrowly converging and widely diverging beams illuminate the road poorly and are liable to dazzle other road users. Adjust the focus of the headlamp immediately if its *beam* is not uniform, is too wide, is of short range, or has a dark centre. To focus the headlamp (where a focusing adjustment is provided), remove the lamp front (already described) and then slacken the screw on the bulb holder clamping clip, illustrated in Fig. 12. The bulb holder can then be moved backwards or forwards on the reflector axis until the headlamp is focused correctly. It is desirable to focus the headlamp against a wall 25–30 feet away from the headlamp. See that the bulb holder clamping screw is firmly retightened after making a final adjustment. For correct bulb renewals, *see* page 25.

Sidecar Lamp (Type LD309). To remove the lamp front and reflector, turn the front to the left, and withdraw. The bulb-holder can then be unclipped from the back of the reflector. When replacing, push the front on so that the arrow stamped on the rim is slightly to the left of the top, and then turn the front until the arrow is at the top of the lamp.

Sidecar Lamp (Type R370). By unscrewing the locating screw at the bottom of the rim, the lamp front and reflector may be removed. Locate the top of the rim first when replacing.

Tail Lamp (Pre-1947). The bulb-holder is mounted on a rubber diaphragm, which prevents road and engine vibration from being transmitted to the filament, thus greatly prolonging its life.

The rear portion of the lamp is removed for bulb replacement by giving it a half-turn to the left, when it becomes detached from its bayonet fixing.

Stop-tail Lamp (1953 Onwards). An entirely new design of stop-tail lamp (Model 525) is fitted to 1953 and later machines, and a reflex red-reflector is also included. To remove the moulded red-plastic cover, it is only necessary to remove two captive screws (*see* Fig. 17). This gives access to the double-filament bulb. One 6-watt filament is provided for

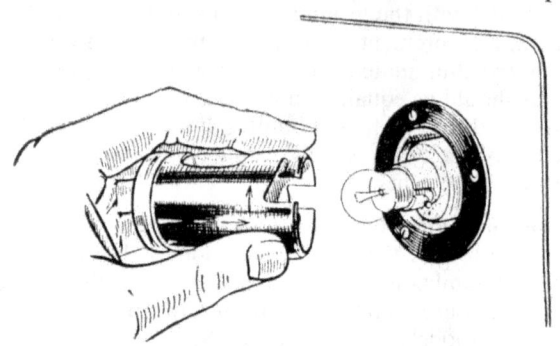

FIG. 16. LUCAS MT211 TAIL LAMP (PRE-1947)
Remove the body of the lamp as indicated by the arrows.

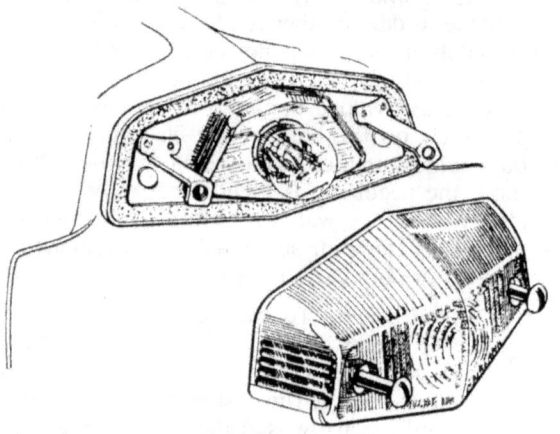

FIG. 17. THE LUCAS 525 STOP-TAIL LAMP (1953 ONWARDS)

the normal rear light and number plate illumination, and an 18-watt filament for the stop light to indicate when the motor-cycle is braking. The bulb holder has staggered slots to ensure the correct fitting of the bulb.

Cleaning Lucas Lamps. Clean the lamp body with a good car polish, and polish the chromium-plated rim with a chamois leather or a soft, dry duster. First wash off all dirt with water. On no account use metal polish

THE LIGHTING EQUIPMENT 25

to clean the reflector which has a transparent and colourless covering (pre-1956). To remove finger marks, polish the reflector with a chamois leather or with a *very* soft dry cloth.

BULB RENEWAL

Replacement of Bulbs (DU142, D142 Headlamps). When this is necessary, use Lucas bulbs. The filaments are arranged to be in focus and give the best results with Lucas reflectors. On the DU142 and D142 Lucas headlamps the main and pilot bulbs (which have a bayonet fixing) are accessible by pushing aside the two securing clips and removing the bracket which secures the bulb holders to the reflector. Make certain that the main bulb is fitted the correct way, i.e. with the dipped beam filament *above* the centre filament. Always focus the headlamp after fitting a new bulb. This applies also to the 1947–9 MU42 and the 1950–2 SSU700P headlamps.

On all headlamps except Lucas type MU42, SSU700P fit a No. 168, 6-volt, 24 watt, double-filament main bulb; and a No. 200, 6-volt, 3 watt, S.B.C. bulb for pilot and sidecar lights (6-volt, 6-watt for tail lamp).

MU42 Headlamp Bulb Replacements. Where a Lucas type MU42 headlamp (*see* Fig. 12) is fitted, the correct bulb replacements are—
Main bulb—6-volt, 24 watt, double-filament Lucas No. 168.
Pilot bulb—6-volt, 3 watt, S.B.C., Lucas No. 200.

SSU700P Headlamp Bulb Replacements. Where a Lucas type SSU700P headlamp without "pre-focus" bulb (*see* Fig. 13) is fitted, the correct bulb replacements are—
Main bulb—6-volt, 30/30 watt, double-filament Lucas No. 169.
Pilot bulb—6-volt, 3 watt, Lucas No. 988.

See that the main bulb is always replaced with the dipped beam filament *above* the centre filament. To assist correct replacement, the bulb is marked "TOP." The bulb holder is secured in position by two spring-loaded pegs and can readily be removed from the rear of the light-unit after detaching the lamp front and Lucas light-unit assembly. The No. 169 Lucas bulb has a bayonet-type fixing for the bulb holder.

Some 1952 and all 1953 and later type SSU700P/1 headlamps are of the "pre-focus" type (*see* Fig. 14) with no focusing adjustment, and they require a No. 312 6-volt, 30/24 watt main bulb which can be fitted in one position only.

The No. 312 "pre-focus" bulb is easy to identify as it has a broad locating flange on its cap. Note that this bulb cannot be fitted to a "focusing" type SSU700P Lucas headlamp.

Referring to Fig. 14, to replace a "pre-focus" bulb, turn the back-shell *anti-clockwise*, pull it off, and remove the bulb from the rear of the reflector. Fit the new bulb (No. 312) in the holder, engage the projections on the inside of the back shell with the slots in the bulb holder, press on the shell, and secure by turning clockwise.

If the pilot bulb of a "pre-focus" SSU700P/1 Lucas headlamp requires renewal, slide out the metal plate above the underslung pilot lens, and fit to it a 6-volt, 3 watt, Lucas No. 988 bulb. See that the metal plate is pressed firmly home afterwards, or it may work free while riding and cause the pilot light to go out, possibly unobserved by the rider.

MCH58 Headlamp Bulb Replacements. Where a Lucas type MCH58 headlamp with "pre-focus" main bulb (*see* Fig. 15) is fitted, the correct bulb replacements are—
  Main bulb—6-volt, 30/24 watt, double-filament Lucas No. 312.
  Pilot bulb—6-volt, 3 watt, Lucas No. 988.

Stop-tail Lamp (1953 Onwards). The correct bulb for a Lucas "525" stop-tail lamp is a Lucas No. 384 6-volt, 6/18 watt double-filament type. See that the bulb is secure in the slotted holder before securing the plastic cover with the two screws.

THE LIGHTING SWITCH AND HORN

The lighting switch and horn seldom develop trouble and are best left well alone. Should trouble occur somewhere in the wiring circuit, the three accompanying wiring diagrams may prove useful, but those who have little electrical knowledge and do not possess a suitable voltmeter are advised to call at a Lucas service depot when any obscure fault in the wiring occurs.

The Switch. All electrical leads to the Lucas headlamp are taken direct to the lighting switch. On the DU142, MU42, SSU700P, SSU700P/1, and MCH58 Lucas headlamps referred to on pages 18–22 the switch and ammeter (also the speedometer, 1956) are mounted on a panel screwed to the headlamp shell.

Before attempting to remove the panel, it is wise to disconnect the appropriate battery lead (*see* page 11). To withdraw the panel from the headlamp it is only necessary to unscrew the three fixing screws. Note that the ends of all cables can be identified by means of coloured sleevings.

The Horn. This should give prolonged service without any attention because it is very carefully adjusted by the makers, and is not subjected to severe stresses. Do not assume that the horn has failed merely because its functioning becomes irregular, or because the horn ceases to vibrate. It is possible that a short-circuit has occurred in the wiring of the horn, a connexion is loose, or the battery is run down. Poor performance can also be caused by a slack horn fixing-bolt, or even by the vibration of some part close to the horn. In this case, hold the horn firmly in the hand by its bracket, and test for note. If unsatisfactory, get the horn examined and adjusted at a Lucas service depot.

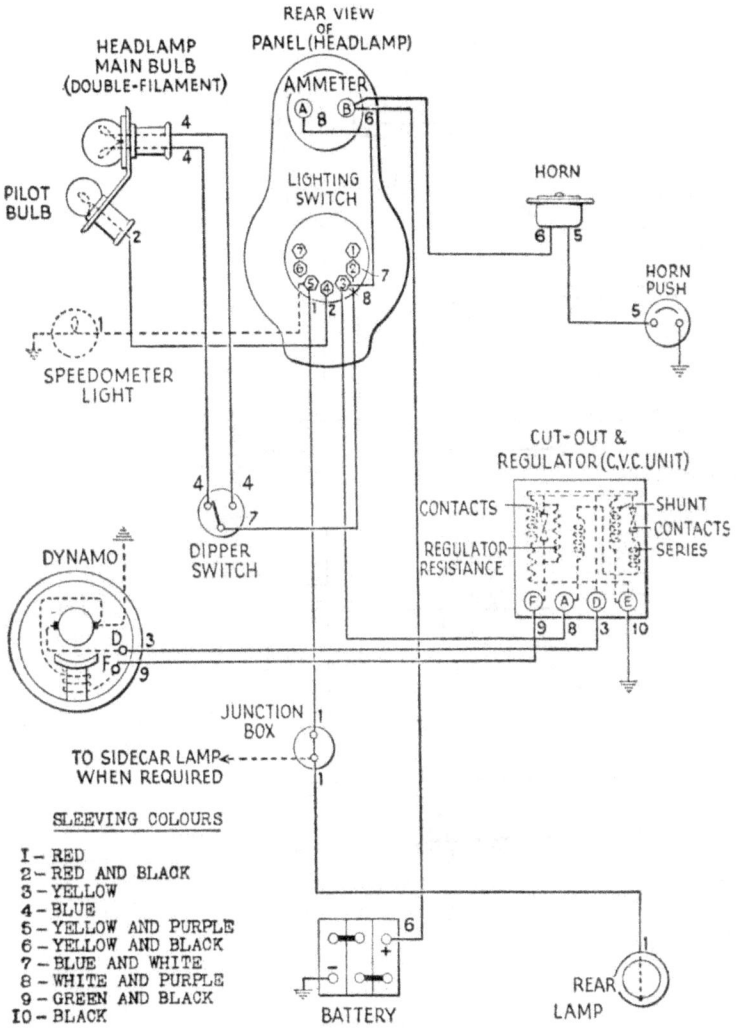

FIG. 18. WIRING DIAGRAM FOR LUCAS "MAGDYNO" LIGHTING EQUIPMENT WITH MU42 OR SSU700P HEADLAMP

(*Joseph Lucas, Ltd.*)

This applies to 1938–52 Nortons with compensated-voltage-control and a "negative earth" system of wiring.

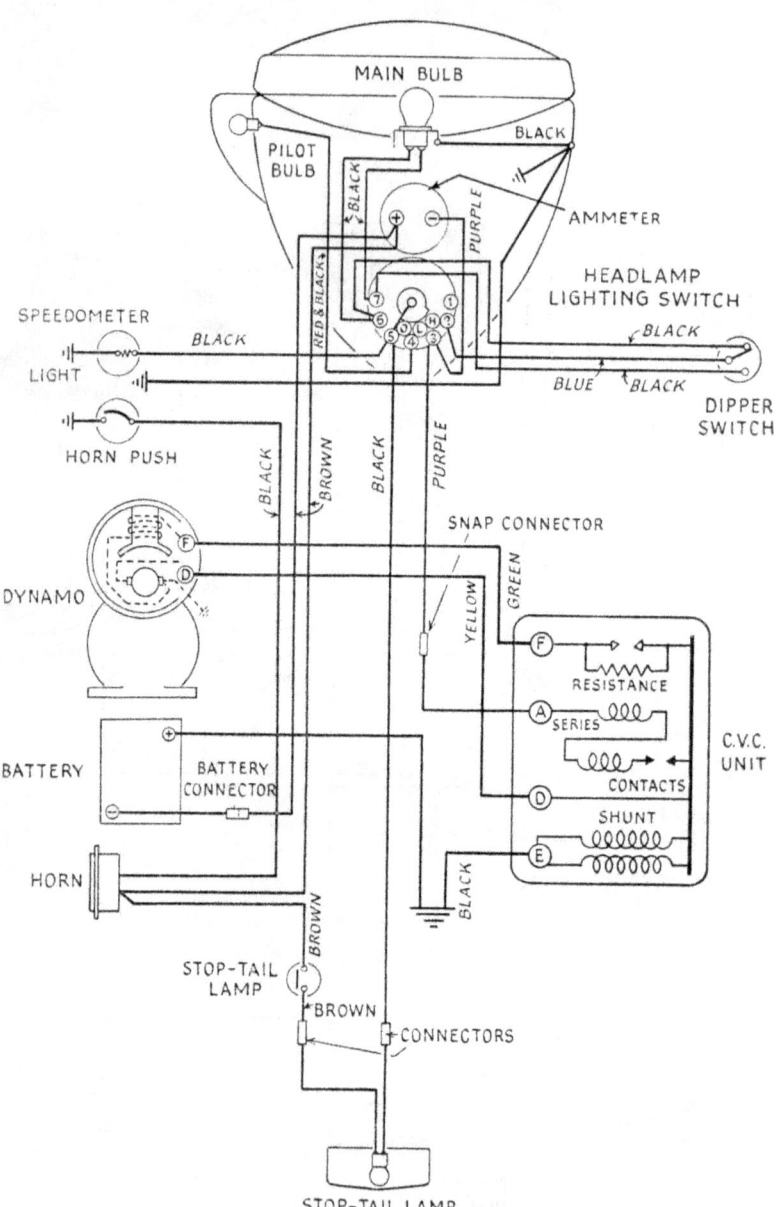

Fig. 19. Wiring Diagram for Lucas "Magdyno" Lighting Equipment with SSU700P/1 Headlamp

This applies to 1953 to 1955 Nortons with compensated-voltage-control and a "positive earth" system of wiring. On 1955 models the lead to the stop-tail lamp is taken from the battery negative instead of from the horn. The battery positive lead has *black* sleeving.

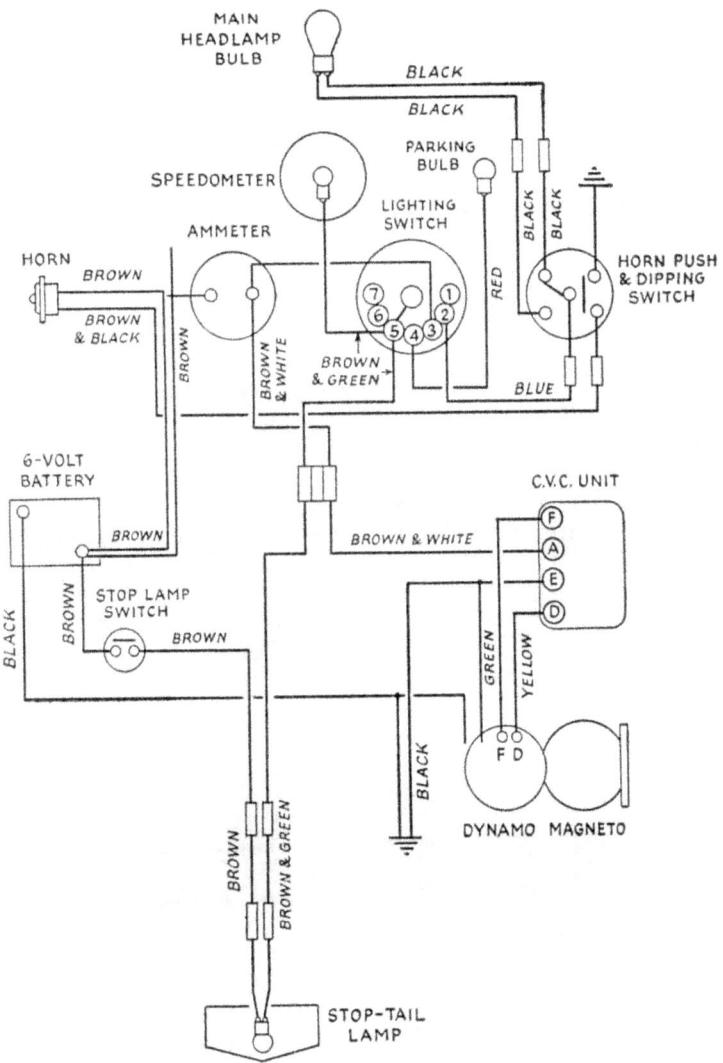

Fig. 20. Wiring Diagram for Lucas "Magdyno" Lighting Equipment with MCH58 Headlamp
This applies to the 1956 Models 19S, ES2, 50.

CHAPTER III

LUBRICATION

LUBRICATION, which consists of maintaining a microscopically thin film of oil on all contacting surfaces, can conveniently be divided into two groups: (*a*) engine lubrication; (*b*) cycle lubrication. On taking over a *new* machine it is only necessary to replenish the oil tank, other lubrication points having been attended to by the makers.

ENGINE LUBRICATION

There are three main parts in the engine where lubrication is vital: (*a*) at that part of the cylinder bore traversed by the piston and the piston rings (which reciprocate at exceptionally high speed); (*b*) the crankshaft assembly, including the two mainshaft bearings, and the big-end and small-end connecting-rod bearings; (*c*) the timing gear and the valve-operating gear.

The Dry-sump Lubrication System (1938-47). This system is very similar to that used up to 1937, except for some detail differences. It is designed to supply automatically the correct amount of oil to all parts under all conditions. The twin gear-type oil pump (Fig. 21) draws oil from the oil

FIG. 21. THE OIL PUMP (S.V. AND O.H.V.) WITH BOTH PAIRS OF GEARS REMOVED

tank and forces it through the restriction jet in the timing-case cover, and through the drilled off-side main-shaft to the big-end bearing of the connecting-rod. Oil exuding from this bearing splash-lubricates the piston and cylinder. An auxiliary oil feed is taken to the rear of the cylinder, and also to the timing gears.

An oil-pressure control valve is included. This has a spring-loaded ball and functions similarly to a "blow off" safety valve. It is incorported in a boss on the inside of the timing-case cover. When the oil pressure causes the valve to lift off its seat, oil passes the valve and is sprayed over the timing gears.

After circulation throughout the engine, the oil collects at the bottom of the crankcase, which has a sludge trap, and is drawn up by the return side

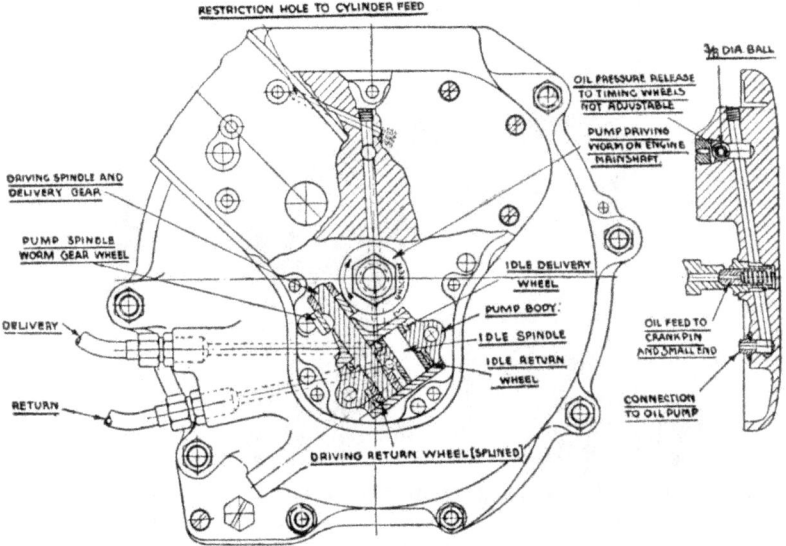

Fig. 22. 1938–47 Dry-sump System (S.V. and O.H.V. Engines)

of the gear pump and pressure-fed back into the oil tank for further circulation. The oil tank has a gauze filter embodied in the pipe union (*see* Fig. 23) and a drain plug is fitted at the base of the tank. Oil mist is employed for the automatic lubrication of the "Magdyno" and secondary chains.

On S.V. engines the valves are completely enclosed in a valve chest and lubricated by a jet with two small orifices protruding from the crankcase. On the O.H.V. engines oil mist is used for lubricating the valve guides, valve ends, and overhead rockers.

The Dry-Sump Lubrication System (1948 Onwards). The D.S. lubrication system varies little from the 1938–47 system, but has an external oil feed to the rocker-box on O.H.V. engines. A gear-type pump similar to that illustrated in Fig. 21 is employed to force oil to: (*a*) the cylinder rear wall; (b) the double-row roller big-end bearing, and (c) the oil-pressure control valve. The return side of the pump picks up surplus oil and returns it to the tank. The gears on this side of the pump are twice as wide as those on the feed side, and therefore, having twice the pumping capacity, keep the crankcase "dry" when the engine is working.

With regard to cylinder lubrication, engine oil supplied by gravity from the tank (assisted by suction from the feed side of the oil pump) is pressure-fed by the delivery side of the oil pump to the crankcase mouth via the timing-case cover ducts, along the cylinder base, and then upwards through

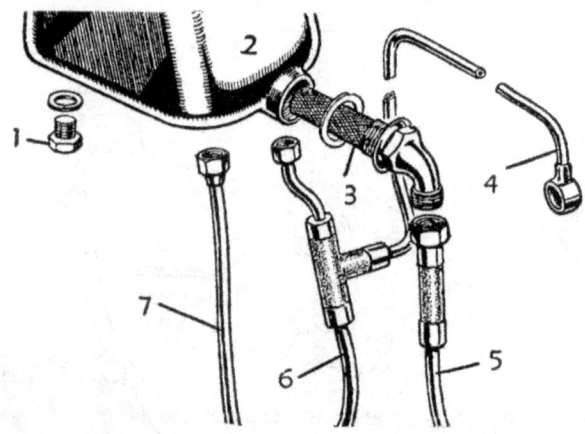

FIG. 23. EXPLODED VIEW SHOWING OIL TANK FILTER AND PIPE CONNEXIONS AT TANK END (PRE-1955)

1. Tank drain-plug and washer.
2. Oil tank.
3. Gauze filter on pipe elbow.
4. Pipe to rocker-box (O.H.V.).
5. Oil-delivery pipe.
6. Oil-return pipe.
7. Tank air-release pipe.

a duct in the wall of the cylinder to the rear of the cylinder bore and the piston.

The big-end roller bearing is lubricated by oil pressure-fed through a timing-case cover duct, through the big-end restriction jet (Fig. 22), through the timing-side main shaft, and then up a duct in the off-side flywheel to the big-end bearing itself.

The oil-pressure control valve functions as a safety valve in the oil circulation system. It has a spring-loaded ball which rises off its seat automatically as soon as the oil pressure reaches a predetermined value. Oil passing the valve becomes sprayed on the timing gears.

Surplus oil from the cylinder drains down the crankcase walls and is conveyed by ducts to the main-shaft bearings, and also to the bearings of the timing gears. The oil pump driving-pinion becomes immersed in oil because of the level of oil accumulated in the timing case. Consequently rotation of the pinion passes oil on to the engine pinion and the two camwheels.

In the case of the Model 16H, and Model 1 S.V. engines, oil reaches the valve chest from the timing case through longitudinal slots in the tappet guides, and all surplus drains into the crankcase.

On the O.H.V. Models 18, 19R, 19S, ES2, 50 a by-pass pipe leads from the oil *return* pipe (*see* Fig. 23) to a banjo union on the rocker-box. Oil is thus fed to the rocker shafts and the ball ends of the overhead rockers. All surplus oil drains down to the crankcase through the two push-rod cover tubes. Surplus from the compartments housing the valve springs drains to the crankcase through holes drilled in the cylinder head and barrel.

The "Magdyno" chain is lubricated by oil passing through the inlet camshaft bush into the "Magdyno" chain case. Surplus oil accumulating in the case drains via the breather pipe. A further timed breather is incorporated in the driving-side main-shaft and releases crankcase pressure through a small hole in the underside of the main-shaft bearing boss. Ejected oil mist is used to lubricate the secondary chain.

Surplus oil throughout the engine drains down to the crankcase base and enters a sludge trap (sludge comes away on removing the drain plug). The oil is then sucked up by the return side of the oil pump and forced back into the oil tank for re-circulation. Only one filter is incorporated in the D.S. lubrication system. It is of the gauze type and, as may be seen in Fig. 23, is sweated into the oil feed pipe elbow screwed into the oil tank.

Suitable Engine Oils. Top-up the oil tank regularly about every 200 miles to the correct level (half to three-quarters full). The brands and grades of engine oils recommended by Norton Motors, Ltd., for all S.V. and O.H.V. Nortons are—
1. Castrol XXL (summer) or XL (winter).
2. Shell X–100 40 (summer) or X–100 30 (winter).
3. Mobiloil BB (summer) or A (winter).
4. B.P. Energol SAE 40 (summer) or Energol SAE 30 (winter).

During the running-in period it is beneficial to mix colloidal graphite with the engine oil (*see* page 9). Note that if this compound is used for a longer period, the amount used should be reduced by half.

Concerning Engine Lubrication. Very little attention indeed is required on 1938 and later dry-sump models, and if the following instructions are carefully followed it is unlikely that any trouble will be experienced. See that the oil tank is always kept half to three-quarters full. Before checking the level in the tank run the engine for a few minutes. By doing this all surplus oil in the crankcase is scavenged by the pump and returned to the tank. It is possible for some oil to siphon through the return gears to the sump after the engine has been allowed to remain stationary for some time.

To check the oil circulation, remove the tank-filler cap and observe the oil being ejected from the oil return pipe. Note that after the engine has been running for several minutes, the oil flow becomes spasmodic because of the greater capacity of the oil-pump return gears, compared with the gears on the feed side.

Upper cylinder lubrication is not necessary but sometimes beneficial. 1938 and later engines have no adjustment provided in the D.S. lubrication system, other than in regard to the oil-pressure control valve.

The Oil-pressure Control Valve. It is inadvisable to remove the ball from the valve unless there is reason to think that the ball is failing to seat, or is

FIG. 24. REMOVING OIL TANK UNION AND FILTER
On later models the filter is withdrawn downwards.

sticking. At the Norton Works the ball spring adjusting-screw is screwed right home and then released 1½ threads. Do not tamper with this adjustment unnecessarily. Incidentally, there is no other adjustment provided in the lubrication system. If for any reason the oil-pressure control valve is dismantled, the correct order of assembly is: the ball itself; the spring; the adjuster nut. Tighten the latter fully and then screw it out 1½ turns. Afterwards lock it with a centre-punch.

Drain the Oil Tank Every 2,000 Miles. On Norton engines with D.S. lubrication, the oil tank should be emptied and flushed out, and the filter cleaned with paraffin at least once every 2,000 miles. In the case of a new or rebored engine do this after the first 500 miles' running.

On 1938 and later models drain the tank by removing the base plug shown at 1 in Fig. 23. Do not lose its washer, and use a large receptacle to avoid an unnecessary mess.

LUBRICATION

Drain Crankcase When Decarbonizing. Drain the crankcase after the first 500 miles and when decarbonizing. Do this when the engine is warm. It is unnecessary on all 1938 and later engines to flush out the crankcase, because a sludge trap is provided. When the crankcase drain-plug is removed, all sludge comes away.

Rocker-box Lubrication. Automatic lubrication of the rocker-box is to be found on all 1938 and later O.H.V. engines, and apart from the optional use of upper-cylinder lubricant mixed with the petrol, no attention by the rider is necessary.

Lubrication of the Lucas "Magdyno." The bearings of the machine are packed with grease before a new model leaves the works, and this is quite sufficient until a complete overhaul is necessary (*see* page 102) when the "Magdyno" unit should be stripped down by a Lucas service agent and the bearings repacked with grease, and the instrument given any other attention that is necessary.

About every 3,000 miles insert a few drops of thin machine-oil on the wick in the contact-breaker base. The wick is carried by a small screw and to remove this screw it is first necessary to remove the spring arm carrying the moving contact (*see* Fig. 41), when the wick screw can be withdrawn.

When replacing the spring arm carrying the outer contact, see that the small backing spring is correctly located on the *outside* of the spring arm, with the curved portion facing *outwards*. Replace the spring washer and securing screw, and tighten the latter firmly.

If occasion is had to remove the complete contact-breaker, it is a good plan to push out the tappet from the contact-breaker body and smear this tappet with a little thin machine-oil.

On some earlier Nortons equipped with dynamos of the Lucas E3HM type, a lubricator will be observed on the commutator driving-end bracket (*see* Fig. 6). A few drops of *thin* oil should be added about every 3,000 miles. All the later "Magdynos" fitted to Nortons embody the Lucas type E3LM dynamo, and this has no lubricator fitted (*see* Fig. 6A).

THE MOTOR-CYCLE PARTS

Four-speed Gearbox Lubrication. Suitable lubricant for the 1938 and later four-speed Norton gearbox is engine oil, preferably of summer grade (*see* page 33). The correct level of lubricant in the four-speed gearbox is such that the layshaft is half submerged (i.e., the gearbox is about *one-third* full). An original charge of ½ pint of engine oil is advised and subsequent topping-up about every 1,000 miles should thereafter be adequate. Do not forget to lubricate the clutch control about once every 1,000 miles.

When topping-up the gearbox, pour engine oil into the filler-plug hole, or use an oil-gun, until the oil level reaches the hole. Rotation with the kick-starter will facilitate replenishment. Drain and refill the gearbox every 5,000 miles. When replenishing the gearbox, always allow ample time for the oil to find its natural level.

The Primary Chain. On 1938–48 models replenish the oil-bath chain case about every 1,000 miles with engine oil (*see* page 33). On 1949 and

Fig. 25. Near-side View of O.H.V. Model Showing Oil-bath Chain Case

A. Inspection cover.
B. Oil-level plug.
C. Nipple for rear-brake pedal.

later models use Wakefield's "Castrolite," Shell X-100 20, B.P. Energol SAE 20, or Mobiloil Arctic. To replenish, remove the inspection cover *A* from the chain case (Fig. 25) and also the oil-level plug *B* from the base of the chain case. Then pour oil through the inspection-cover hole until it

FIG. 26. WHEN AND WHERE TO LUBRICATE (1947 ONWARDS)

The above chart showing a 1954 Model ES2 applies in general to all 1947 and subsequent Norton singles. See page 39 for the lubrication of the rear springing (ES2, 19R, 19S, 50) and the saddle-nose pin.

KEY TO FIG. 26

Item No.	Description of Item	Lubrication, etc., Required	Page Ref.
1	Oil tank	Every 200 miles inspect oil level and top-up as required. Every 2,000 miles change the oil and clean the filter.	33, 34
2	Engine crankcase	When decarbonizing, drain the crankcase	35
3	Lucas "Magdyno"	Every 3,000 miles add a few drops of thin oil to the contact-breaker wick.	35
4	Gearbox	Every 1,000 miles top-up with engine oil.	35
5	Primary chain	Every 1,000 miles top-up oil-bath to the level of the level-plug orifice. Every 10,000 miles drain and replenish with new oil.	36
6	Secondary chain	Every 1,000 miles grease thoroughly. Every 3,500 miles remove, clean, and grease.	38
7	Front forks {telescopic type	Every 5,000 miles drain completely and replenish with ¼ pint of new damping oil.	38
	girder type	Every 2,000 miles apply grease gun to fork spindle nipples.	38
8	Steering head	Every 2,000 miles apply grease gun to both nipples.	38
9	Handlebar controls	Weekly apply a few spots of oil to control levers and exposed cables.	39
10	Front and rear hubs	Every 1,000 miles apply grease gun to both hub nipples.	39
11	Brake cam spindles	Every 2,000 miles grease both nipples with grease gun.	39
12	Front-brake cable	Weekly oil the ends of exposed portion.	39
13	Rear-brake pedal	Every 2,000 miles apply grease gun to the nipple.	39
14	Speedometer-drive gearbox	Every 2,000 miles grease the nipple with grease gun	39

reaches the oil-level plug hole with the motor-cycle upright. Drain and refill (½ pint) every 10,000 miles.

The Secondary Chain. Brush on graphite grease every 1,000 miles. Engine oil can be used for the chain also, and in this case the best method of lubricating the chain is to rotate it, with the wheel, and apply an oil-gun or an oil-can to the lower chain run. See that the oil is falling upon the bearing surfaces and not merely on the rollers, and lubricate whenever the chain seems to be running dry. If chain lubrication is insufficient, undue wear of the chain and sprockets will occur, and the transmission may become somewhat harsh.

From time to time (say, every 3,500 miles) remove the chain and submerge it in paraffin. If the chain is allowed to soak well, all the dirt will be extracted. Hang the chain up to dry and replace it. Before doing this, however, it is a good plan to immerse the chain in a receptacle containing a quantity of warm chain lubricant containing graphite. This will penetrate to all the bearing surfaces.

On 1938 and later Nortons the secondary chain is automatically lubricated by oil mist from the crankcase breather, but it also requires greasing about every 1,000 miles.

The Steering Head. Grease the ball bearings in the steering head every 2,000 miles by applying the grease-gun to the nipples.

Suitable Greases. Suitable greases to use for all grease-gun points on the machine are: Wakefield's Castrolease Heavy, Shell Retinax C.D., B.P. Energrease C3, or Mobiloil Hub Grease. When using the grease-gun, make sure that it is adequately filled, and try it out before applying it.

Grease Girder-type Forks. On 1938–46 models provided with girder-type front forks it is advisable to apply the grease-gun to the nipples for the fork spindles about every 2,000 miles.

Replenishing the Telescopic Front Forks. "Roadholder" telescopic-type front forks with hydraulic damping are fitted as standard to all 1947 and later Nortons. These require to be replenished with damping oil about every 5,000 miles. Suitable damping oils are: Wakefield's "Castrolite," Shell X–100 20, or B.P. Energol SAE 20.

To replenish the forks, first remove the hexagon-headed filler plug from the top of each fork leg. Then remove the drain plug from each fork-end and allow all damping oil to drain out. Complete draining is assisted by operating the forks manually a few times. Replace the two drain plugs and replenish each fork leg with a measured *quarter of a pint* of one of the above-mentioned damping oils. Afterwards operate the forks several times to eliminate air locks, and finally replace the two filler plugs.

LUBRICATION

Wheel Hubs. On both the front and rear wheels, nipples are provided, and the hubs should each be injected with 3–4 strokes of the grease-gun about every 1,000 miles. Do not use excessive grease, or it may get on the brake linings and reduce brake efficiency. Use one of the greases mentioned on the opposite page. It is most important to keep the bearings of all wheels well greased, as they perform heavy duties. On a sidecar outfit, do not forget to grease the bearings of the sidecar wheel.

Brakes. Grease the brake pedal shaft (*C*, Fig. 25), and the brake-cam spindles every 2,000 miles. Appropriate nipples are provided. Oil the exposed front-brake cable and the rear-brake rod joints weekly.

Control Levers. Apply the oil-can weekly to the cables where they are apt to bind on the control mechanism on the handlebars. Oil all linkage pins and also the nipples. When fitting new cables and casings, charge the latter with grease. A length of rubber tube can be used in conjunction with the grease-gun to inject grease.

The Rear Springing. On 1938–52 models with rear suspension-units of the type shown in Fig. 84, inject some grease every 1,000 miles into the two nipples. On 1953 and later models with "swinging arm" rear suspension (*see* Fig. 85) no lubrication or other maintenance is necessary. The oil-damped units are leak-proof, and normally no attempt should be made to dismantle, drain, or replenish the suspension units. Do not lubricate the "swinging arm" pivot which has "Silentbloc" bushes (*see* page 141).

Miscellaneous. Every 2,000 miles grease the speedometer-drive gear-box, and oil the saddle-nose pin (unless a dual seat is fitted).

CHAPTER IV

THE AMAL CARBURETTOR

ALL Nortons are sent out from the works with their carburettors carefully tuned and with jet sizes giving the best all-round performance. It is not wise to alter the maker's setting, but sometimes it is disturbed and requires adjustment. The carburettor fitted to all 1938 and later Norton engines is of the two-lever needle-jet type, the mixture at slow or idling speeds being controlled by a readily adjustable pilot jet, whilst at higher speeds the mixture is controlled by means of a needle attached to the throttle slide and working in a restriction jet.

HOW IT WORKS (1938-54)

Referring to Fig. 27, showing a view of the standard carburettor, A is the carburettor body or mixing chamber, the upper part of which has a throttle valve B, with taper needle C attached by a needle clip. The throttle valve regulates the quantity of mixture supplied to the engine. Passing through the throttle valve is the air valve D, independently operated, and serving the purpose of obstructing the main air passage for starting and mixture regulation. Fixed to the underside of the mixing chamber by the union nut E is the jet block F, and interposed between them is a fibre washer to ensure a petrol-tight joint. On the upper part of the jet block is the adaptor body H, forming a clean through-way. Integral with the jet block is the pilot jet J, supplied through the passage K. The adjustable pilot air-intake L communicates with a chamber, from which issues the pilot outlet M and the by-pass N. A throttle-stop screw (Fig. 28) is fitted on the mixing chamber, by which the position of the throttle valve for tick-over is regulated independently of the cable adjustment. The needle jet O is screwed in the underside of the jet block, and carries at its bottom end the main jet P. Both these jets are removable when the jet plug Q, which bolts the mixing chamber and the float chamber together, is removed. The float chamber, which has bottom feed, consists of a cup R, supplied with petrol through union S. It contains the float T and the needle valve U held by the clip V. The float-chamber cover W has a lock screw X for security. Lock-ring Z (held by clip $Z1$) holds the mixing-chamber cap Y.

The petrol tap having been turned on, petrol will flow past the needle valve U until the quantity of petrol in the chamber R is sufficient to raise the float T, when the needle valve U will prevent a further supply entering the float chamber until some in the chamber has already been used up by the engine. The float chamber having filled to its correct level, the fuel

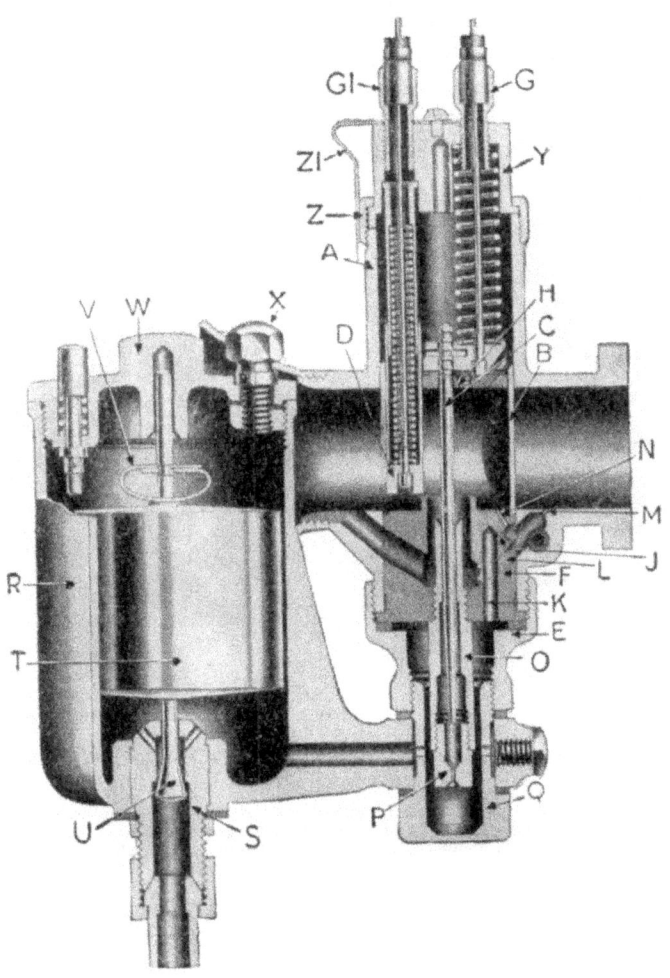

Fig. 27. Sectional View of Two-lever Needle-jet Standard Amal Carburettor (1938–54)

On all 1938–54 S.V. and O.H.V. Nortons this Amal carburettor is secured to the induction stub by means of a clip. Other views of the carburettor are shown on pages 43, 53.

passes along the passages through the diagonal holes in the jet plug *Q*, when it will be in communication with the main jet *P* and the pilot feedhole *K;* the level in the needle and pilot jets is, obviously, the same as that maintained in the float chamber.

Imagine the throttle valve *B* very slightly open. As the piston descends, a partial vacuum is created in the carburettor, causing a rush of air through the pilot air hole *L*, and drawing fuel from the pilot jet *J*. The mixture of

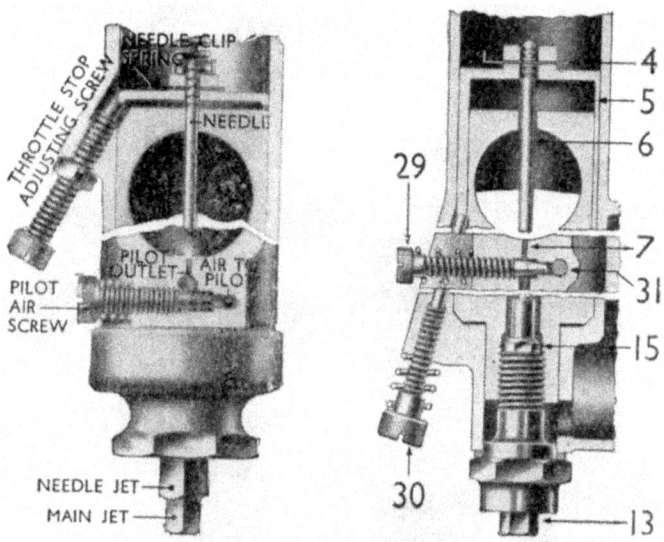

FIG. 28. ARRANGEMENT OF THROTTLE-STOP AND PILOT-AIR ADJUSTING SCREWS

On the left is shown the arrangement on the 1938–9 carburettor, and on the right the arrangement of the 1955 and later "monobloc" instrument. For key to numbered parts, see page 46. Fig. 29 shows the arrangement on the 1946–54 carburettor.

air and fuel is admitted to the engine through the pilot outlet *M*. The quantity of mixture capable of being passed by the pilot outlet *M* is insufficient to run the engine. This mixture also carries excess of fuel. Consequently, before a combustible mixture is admitted, the throttle valve *B* must be slightly raised, admitting a further supply of air from the main air-intake. The farther the throttle valve is opened, the less will be the depression on the outlet *M*, but, in turn, a higher depression will be created on the by-pass *N*, and the pilot mixture will flow from this passage as well as from the outlet *M*.

The mixture supplied by the pilot and by-pass system is supplemented at about one-eighth throttle by fuel from the main jet *P*, the throttle valve cut-away determining the mixture strength from here to one-quarter throttle. Proceeding up the throttle range, mixture control by the needle position occurs from one-quarter to three-quarters throttle, and from this point the main jet is the only regulation.

The air valve *D*, which is cable-operated on the two-lever carburettor, has the effect of obstructing the main through-way and, in consequence,

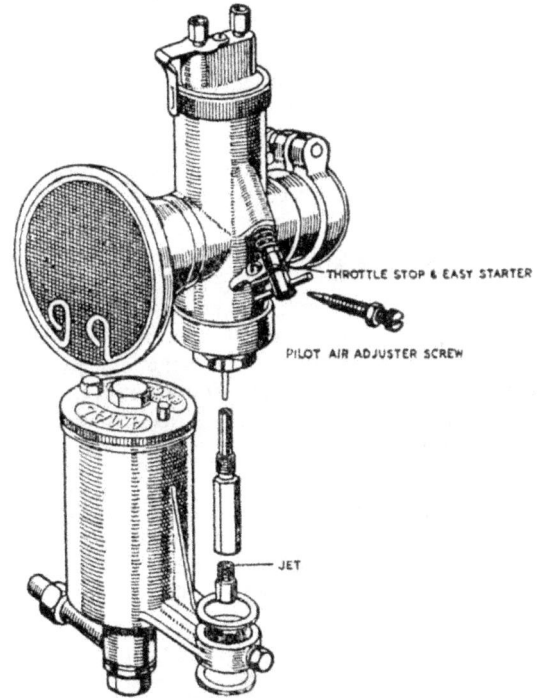

Fig. 29. Partly Exploded View of 1946–54 Amal Carburettor, Showing Throttle Stop and Easy Starter

The jet plug (*see* Fig. 34) is not shown.

increasing the depression on the main jet, enriching the mixture. Two cable adjusters *G*, *G*1 are provided.

The Throttle Stop. The throttle-stop screw is normally adjusted to prop the throttle slide open sufficiently to enable the engine to tick-over nicely when the twist-grip is closed.

The design of the throttle-stop screw on the carburettor fitted to 1938–9 S.V. and O.H.V. and 1955–6 O.H.V. Nortons is shown in Fig. 28. On 1946–54 models a combined throttle-stop and easy starter (*see* Fig. 29) replaces the earlier design. The correct adjustment of the throttle stop and the use of the easy starter device are explained on pages 50 and 51 respectively.

The Pilot Air Screw. This controls the suction imposed on the pilot jet by controlling the volume of air which mixes with the fuel. It controls the strength of the mixture for "idling" and also for initial throttle openings (up to one-eighth throttle, *see* Fig. 33).

The Main Jet. This regulates the fuel supply at throttle openings exceeding three-quarters full open. At smaller openings of the throttle, the fuel supplied passes through the main jet, but the amount is decreased owing to the needle in the needle-jet having a controlling effect. The main jet is screwed into the needle-jet and can readily be detached after removing the jet plug (*Q* in Fig. 27). Referring to Fig. 28, to remove the main jet, hold the needle-jet with one spanner, and with another unscrew the main jet.

Each Amal main jet is numbered and calibrated so that its precise discharge is known. It thus follows that any two main jets having the same number are identical in all respects. The larger the jet, the higher is its number. If a larger size jet is needed, on no account attempt to ream the existing jet, but obtain a new one of larger size. Recommended jet sizes are given in Tables I–III.

The Needle and Needle-jet. The jet needle is attached to, and moves with, the throttle slide. Being tapered, it permits more or less fuel to pass through the needle-jet as the throttle is opened, or closed, respectively. This applies throughout the range of throttle openings, except at nearly full throttle and when "idling." The needle-jet is of a specified size, and normally it should not be changed except when going over to alcohol fuels for racing.

As may be seen in Fig. 28, the position of the taper needle, relative to the throttle opening, can be adjusted according to the mixture required, by securing the needle to the throttle with the needle spring-clip in a particular groove, *five* of which are provided. Position No. 3, for example, means the third groove *from the top*. At throttle openings from one-quarter to three-quarters open, raising the needle enriches the mixture, while lowering the needle weakens it. The needle itself is made in *one size only*.

The Throttle-valve Cut-away. The throttle valve on the atmospheric side is cut away, and this affects the depression on the main fuel supply. The cut-away provides a means of tuning between the pilot and needle-jet range of throttle opening. The actual amount of cut-away is denoted by a number marked on the throttle slide. Thus 6/4 means a throttle type 6 with a No. 4 cut-away. A throttle with a larger cut-away (say, 6/5) *weakens* the mixture. A smaller cut-away, on the other hand, makes the mixture *richer*.

HOW IT WORKS (1955 ONWARDS)

Details of the Amal "monobloc" carburettor are shown in Figs. 28 and 30–2, and the accompanying key to these four sectional views indicates all the essential parts. Basically, the carburettor works on the same general principles as the earlier type with a vertical and separate float chamber, non-detachable pilot jet, and needle-jet of the non-compensating type.

Referring to Figs. 30–2, the float 27 maintains a constant level of petrol in the needle-jet 15 and the pilot jet 9, and it cuts off the petrol supply when the engine stops.

The selection of the appropriate jet sizes and main choke bore ensures the proper atomizing and proportioning of the petrol and air sucked into the engine. The air valve is normally kept fully raised and the throttle valve (controlled by the handlebar twist-grip) controls the volume of mixture and therefore the power; at all throttle openings a correct mixture is automatically obtained. The carburettor operates in four stages.

When opening the throttle from the fully closed position to one-eighth open (for idling) the mixture is supplied by the pilot jet, and mixture strength is determined by the setting of the knurled pilot-air adjusting screw (*see* Fig. 28). To facilitate adjustment of this screw a coil spring is used instead of a lock-nut. As the throttle is opened farther the main-jet system comes into action, the mixture being augmented from the main jet 13 via the pilot by-pass 8.

The amount of cut-away on the atmospheric side of the throttle valve regulates the petrol-air ratio between one-eighth and one-quarter throttle. The needle-jet 15 and the jet needle 6 take over mixture regulation between one-quarter and three-quarter throttle, and mixture strength is determined by the vertical position of the needle in the clip 4 attached to the throttle valve 5. When the throttle is opened beyond three-quarter, the mixture strength is decided only by the size of the main jet.

Note that the main jet 13 does not spray petrol direct into the carburettor mixing-chamber but petrol discharges through the needle-jet into the primary air chamber. From there it enters the main air choke through the primary air choke 34. The latter has a compensating action in conjunction with "bleed" holes 33 in the needle-jet 15, which serve the double purpose of air compensating the mixture from the needle-jet and allowing the fuel to form a well outside and around the needle-jet. This is always available for snap acceleration. Pilot-jet and main-jet behaviour are not affected by this two-way compensation governing only acceleration and normal cruising.

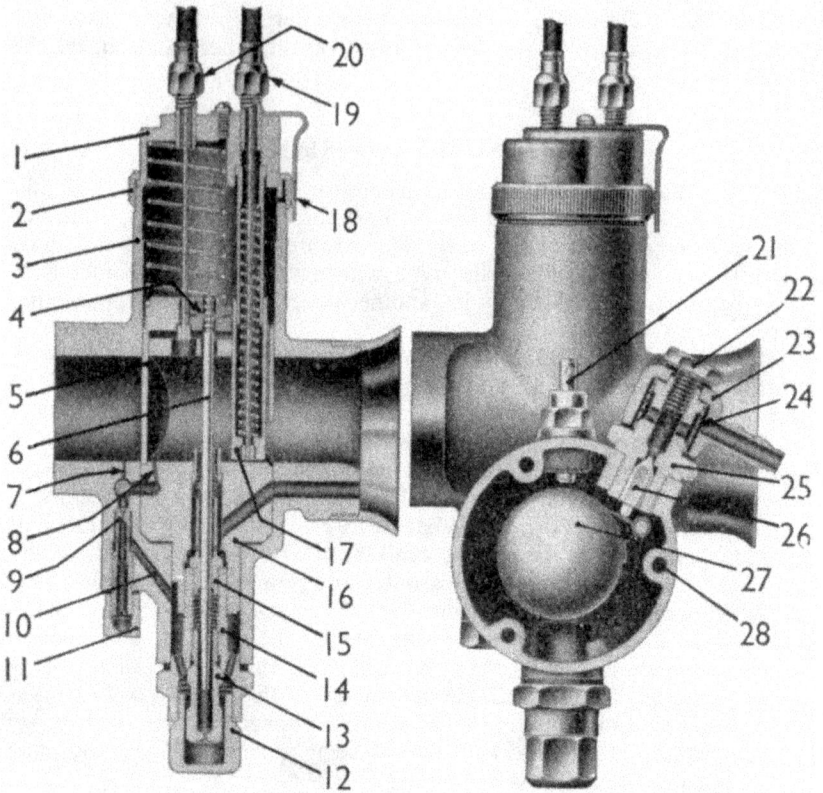

FIGS. 30, 31. SECTIONS THROUGH (LEFT) MIXING CHAMBER AND (RIGHT) FLOAT CHAMBER OF AMAL "MONOBLOC" CARBURETTOR (1955 ONWARDS)

KEY TO FIGS. 28, 30–2

1. Mixing-chamber top.
2. Mixing-chamber cap.
3. Body of carburettor.
4. Jet-needle clip.
5. Throttle valve.
6. Jet needle.
7. Pilot outlet.
8. Pilot by-pass.
9. Pilot jet.
10. Feed to pilot jet.
11. Pilot-jet cover nut.
12. Main-jet cover.
13. Main jet.
14. Main-jet holder.
15. Needle-jet.
16. Jet block.
17. Air valve.
18. Retaining spring for 2.
19. Cable adjuster (air).
20. Cable adjuster (throttle).
21. Tickler.
22. Banjo bolt.
23. Banjo.
24. Filter gauze.
25. Needle seating.
26. Float-chamber needle.
27. Float (hinged).
28. Float-chamber cover screws.
29. Pilot-air adjusting screw.
30. Throttle-stop adjusting screw.
31. Air passage to pilot jet.
32. Feed holes in 9.
33. "Bleed" holes in 15.
34. Primary air choke.
35. Primary air passage.
36. Throttle-valve cut-away.

TUNING THE CARBURETTOR (1938 ONWARDS)

The correct Amal carburettor settings for all 1938–56 Norton single-cylinder S.V. and O.H.V. models are given in Tables I–III. Do not alter these settings (decided by the makers after careful deliberation) without very good reasons.

Note that it is desirable to obtain a slightly weak mixture consistent with good slow-running; an excessively rich slow-running mixture causes a tendency for the engine to run on the pilot jet under normal running

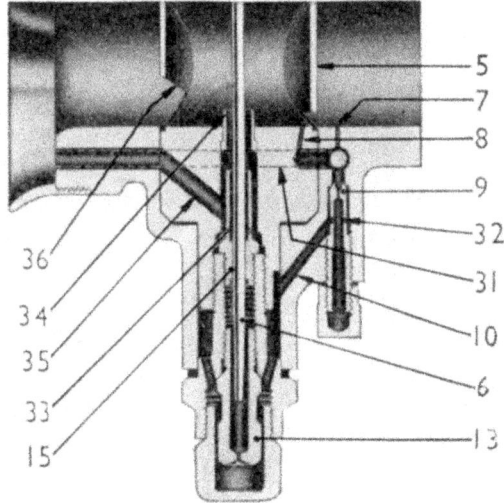

FIG. 32. DIAGRAMMATIC SECTION THROUGH AMAL "MONOBLOC" CARBURETTOR (1955 ONWARDS)

Illustrating only the lower half of the throttle chamber and the internal primary air passages to the main jet and pilot system. The throttle valve is shown slightly open.

conditions. The effect of this is to increase the fuel consumption. To modify the strength of the running mixture, it is necessary to make an adjustment to the position of the jet needle in the throttle valve, or else to alter the size of the main jet.

Colour of the Exhaust Flame. Where the carburettor is correctly tuned, there should be no evidence of black smoke. The combustion of fuel is complete and carbon formation almost non-existent. If the mixture is right, the exhaust flame is of a *whitish-blue* colour.

If the mixture is weak, the colour of the exhaust flame is *light blue*. If, on the other hand, the mixture is excessively rich, the flame is of a characteristic *yellow* colour, and some *black* smoke is generally present. Note that the above references to exhaust flames imply exhaust flames observed at an *open* exhaust port.

Tuning Procedure. If the carburettor setting (*see* Tables I–III) does not give complete satisfaction for particular requirements, there are four

TABLE I
CARBURETTOR SETTINGS FOR S.V. AND O.H.V. MODELS (1938–9)

Model (Norton)	Carb. Type Number	Main Jet Size	Throttle Valve	Needle Position
16H	70/011	170	6/4	Middle
1	76/011	160	6/5	Middle
18	76/022	160	6/4	Middle
19	76/022	160	6/4	Middle
20	76/022	200	6/4	Middle
50	76/012	170	6/4	Middle
55	76/012	170	6/4	Middle
ES2	76/022	160	6/4	Middle

TABLE II
CARBURETTOR SETTINGS FOR S.V. AND O.H.V. MODELS (1946–7)

Model (Norton)	Carb. Type Number	Main Jet Size	Throttle Valve	Needle Position
16H	276 AT	170	6/4	Middle
1	276 AT	160	6/5	Middle
18	276 AU	160	6/4	Middle
ES2	276 AU	160	6/4	Middle

separate ways of rectifying matters as given herewith, and the adjustments should be made in this order—
  1. Main jet ($\frac{3}{4}$ to full throttle).
  2. Pilot air adjustment (closed to $\frac{1}{8}$ throttle).
  3. Throttle-valve cut-away on the air intake side ($\frac{1}{8}$ to $\frac{1}{4}$ throttle).
  4. Needle position ($\frac{1}{4}$ to $\frac{3}{4}$ throttle).

The diagram (Fig. 33) clearly indicates the part of the throttle range over which each adjustment is effective.

THE AMAL CARBURETTOR

The carburettor is, throughout the throttle range, entirely automatic, and the air lever should be kept wide open, except for starting from cold and until the engine has warmed up properly. It is assumed that normal petrol is used for tuning, which should be done in the sequence described below. Throttle openings to be used in the five tuning operations are those indicated in Fig. 33. By following these tuning instructions (which have been recommended by Amal, Ltd.) you will be assured of the most satisfactory performance with maximum economy of fuel. For tuning purposes it is advisable to start up on a quiet road having a slight up-gradient, so as to impose a small load on the engine.

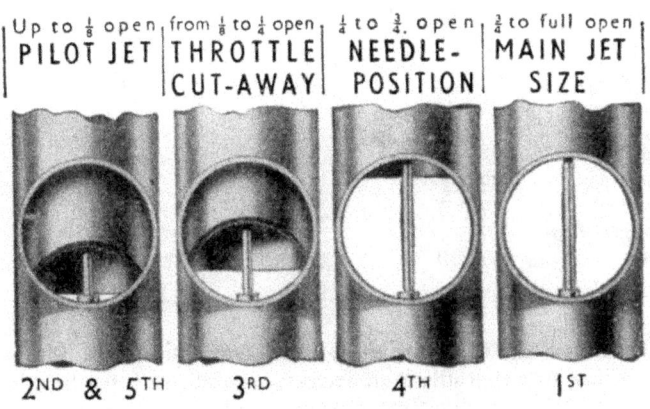

FIG. 33. RANGE AND SEQUENCE OF TUNING—
AMAL CARBURETTOR

1. To Check Size of the Main Jet. Accelerate up to full throttle and carefully note the response of the engine to twist-grip action. Should power output appear better with the air lever very slightly closed or with the throttle not completely open, this indicates that the main jet is too small, and the next larger size should be tried. Similarly, if there is a tendency for the engine to run "heavily" on full throttle, this denotes that the main jet is too large and the next smaller size should be experimented with.*

If tuning for speed, be careful to choose a main jet of size sufficient to maintain the engine in a cool condition. Make a run at high speed, pull up, and stop the engine immediately. Remove the sparking plug and closely inspect it. If the business end of the plug is sooty, the mixture is too rich. Should the body be dry grey in colour, the mixture is on the weak side, and a larger size jet is required.

* Different size jets are obtainable from Amal spares stockists, or from Amal, Ltd., Holdford Road, Witton, Birmingham, 6.

With a properly proportioned mixture, the plug body should have a bright black appearance. Also, when running, observe the sound of the exhaust; it should be crisp and have no trace of "woolliness." Black smoke at the exhaust shows that the mixture is much too rich.

TABLE III
CARBURETTOR SETTINGS FOR S.V. AND O.H.V. MODELS (1948–56)

Model (Norton)	Carb. Type Number	Main Jet Size	Throttle Valve	Needle Position
16H (1948–54)	276 AT	160	6/5	Middle
1 (1948–9)	276 AT	160	6/5	Middle
1 (1950–4)	276 AT	170	6/4	Middle
18 (1948–54)	276 AU	160	6/4	Middle
ES2 (1948–54)	276 AU	160	6/4	Middle
ES2 (1955–6)	376/17	270	376/4	Middle
19R, 19S (1955–6)	376/17	270	376/4	Middle
50 (1956)	376/19	210	376/3½	No. 2

2A. To Adjust the Pilot Jet (1938–9 and 1955 Onwards). Start up the engine. Allow it to run idle at an excessive speed, with the throttle twist-grip closed and the throttle slide abutting the throttle-stop screw (Fig. 28). Open the air lever wide open and retard the ignition lever to obtain the best slow-running.

Loosen the nut (1938–9 models) on the throttle-stop screw, and unscrew the latter until the engine slows up and begins to stall. Then screw the pilot-air screw in or out as required to enable the engine to run regularly and faster. To weaken the mixture, screw the pilot-air adjuster screw *outwards*.

Next gently lower the throttle-stop screw until the engine again begins to falter. Now lock the throttle-stop screw with the lock-nut (1938–9 models) and commence to readjust the pilot-air adjuster screw to obtain the optimum slow-running. Should this second adjustment cause the engine to tick-over at an excessive speed, repeat the adjustment a third time. When perfect slow-running has been obtained, tighten the lock-nut (1938–9 models) on the throttle-stop screw without disturbing the position of the screw. The foregoing adjustment is most important.

2B. To Adjust the Pilot Jet (1946–54 Models). The procedure is fundamentally similar to that recommended for 1938–9 and 1955–6 models, though a little different because of the altered throttle-stop design.

THE AMAL CARBURETTOR

Start up the engine and allow it to tick-over rather fast with the handlebar air lever wide open and the ignition lever adjusted to give smooth running. Screw the pilot-air adjuster screw (*see* Fig. 29) fully home while carefully closing the throttle twist-grip. The engine should now run heavily and begin to "eight-stroke."

Slowly unscrew the pilot-air adjuster screw, when the engine revolutions will rise, necessitating further closing of the throttle. Repeat the adjustment until by a combination of throttle and pilot-air adjustment, perfect slow-running is obtained.

Now proceed to adjust the throttle stop and easy starter, so that it is possible to shut the twist-grip completely without stopping the engine.

Referring to Fig. 29, with a screwdriver loosen the small locking screw, and while holding with the left thumb the shaped stop-piece against the body of the mixing chamber, turn the throttle-stop screw tommy-bar until you hear a slight increase in engine revolutions. Then turn the tommy-bar back until the engine resumes its original speed, and retighten the locking screw. The easy starter device is now set for obtaining a quick start (*see* page 7).

3. The Throttle Cut-away. Should appreciable spitting-back at the carburettor occur on accelerating from rest* with the engine idling, stop the machine and slightly enrich the mixture by screwing the pilot-air screw in approximately *half a turn*. If this does not effect the desired result, screw it back to its former position and fit a throttle slide having a smaller cut-away.

If there is no spitting-back but the engine jerks under load, this shows an over-rich mixture, and the remedy is to fit a throttle slide with larger cut-away, or else to lower the throttle needle one notch.

4. The Jet-needle Position. The tapered jet-needle influences a wide range of throttle openings and affects acceleration. Check performance with the needle in as low a position as possible, i.e. with the clip in the groove nearest the end of the needle. If acceleration declines, and improves by partially closing the air lever, raise the position of the needle by two grooves. If a marked improvement is thereby obtained, try the effect of lowering the needle, by one groove, and leave it in the position where the best performance is obtained.

It should be noted that if the mixture is still excessively rich with the needle clip in groove No. 1 (nearest the end), wear of the needle-jet has probably occurred and renewal of the jet is called for. The needle itself is of stainless steel and wear does not take place, even after a big mileage.

* Rev the engine up and down sharply several times and note whether the exhaust is nice and crisp, with no "flat spots" as the twist-grip is rotated. It is essential to obtain good acceleration as well as good tick-over.

5. Verify the Idling Adjustment. Also make any final small adjustment to obtain a perfectly smooth tick-over, neither too fast nor too slow.

Possible Causes of Bad Slow-running. If it is found impossible to obtain good slow-running by making the pilot air adjustment as described in paragraph 2 on page 50, it is possible there are air leaks, due to a poor joint at the carburettor attachment to the cylinder and/or a worn inlet valve guide. Badly seating valves will also weaken the mixture. Defects in the ignition system may also be responsible for poor tick-over. The sparking plug may be oily, or the points set too close (*see* page 63). Possibly the spark is excessively advanced or the contact-breaker needs attention (*see* page 66). Examine the slip-ring for oil and see that the pick-up brush is bedding down and in good condition. Also examine the h.t. cable for signs of shorting.

The Pilot Jet Obstructed. If the pilot-jet adjustment does not obtain the desired results and the engine will not idle nicely with the throttle almost closed, the air lever adjusted wide open, and the ignition half to two-thirds advanced, it is possible that the pilot jet is obstructed. The jet on 1938–54 models is acually a duct drilled in the jet block, is very small, and can easily become choked.

To gain access to the pilot jet on 1938–54 models, remove the jet plug and float chamber (*see* Fig. 34), and detach the jet block by pushing or tapping it out of the carburettor body. The pilot jet can then be cleared by blowing. On 1955 and later models it is only necessary to remove the pilot-jet cover nut 11 below the choke body (*see* Fig. 30) and unscrew the pilot jet for inspection and cleaning. The correct jet is a No. 30.

High Fuel Consumption. If, in spite of careful checking of the tuning of the carburettor, high fuel consumption continues, it is likely that one or more of the following causes is responsible. Late ignition timing will eat into your petrol supplies quickly. The same applies to poor engine compression due to badly fitting piston rings or badly seated valves. Also take into consideration the question of flooding due to a tilted carburettor (where it has a clip-fixing), or a faulty float or needle (*see* Fig. 35), air leakage at the joint between the carburettor and engine, or weak valve springs. See that no wastage is caused by slack petrol-pipe union nuts.

MAINTENANCE

Stripping Down 1938–54 Carburettor. Periodical cleaning is necessary to maintain efficient functioning of the carburettor. It is best to disconnect the petrol pipe and remove the carburettor from the induction stub after slackening the clip securing-screw. Referring to Fig. 27, unscrew the mixing chamber lock ring Z, held by clip $Z1$; detach the mixing chamber cap Y. Then pull out the air valve D and the throttle valve B, with the jet

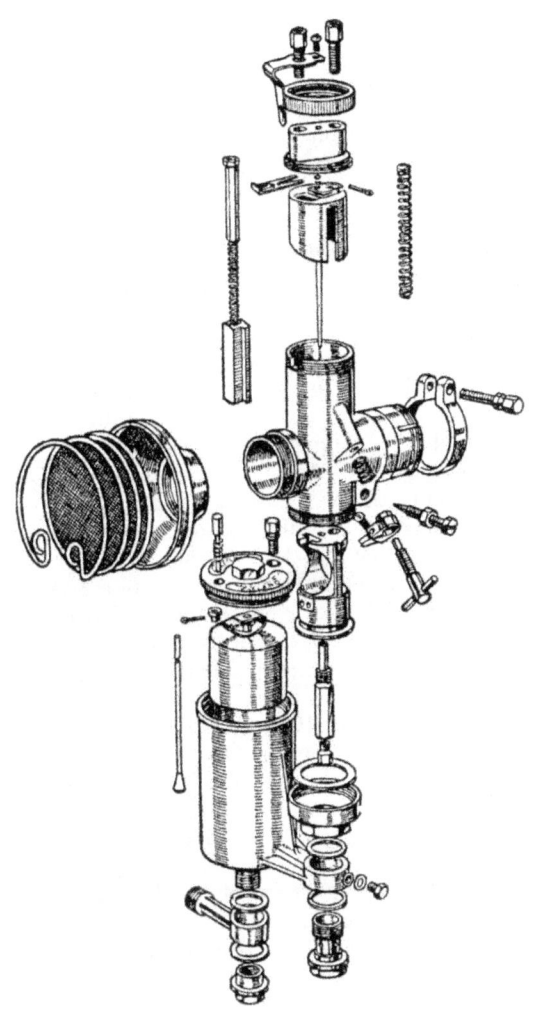

Fig. 34. Exploded view of standard Amal Needle-jet Carburettor showing all components (1946–54)

(*Norton Motors, Ltd.*)

Other views of the Amal carburettor are shown in Figs. 27 and 29. Fig. 29 does not show the jet plug.

needle C attached. To inspect the two valves, or slides, and the jet needle, it is not *necessary* to detach the two slides from the control cables.

Should you desire to detach the air valve D from the control cable $G1$, compress the spring and release the nipple from the base of the slide. To remove the throttle valve B from the control cable G, compress the spring and permit the cable nipple to vacate the hole in which it seats. Then release the spring and allow the nipple to pass through the larger hole.

In order to remove the taper jet-needle C from the drum-shaped throttle slide, remove the spring clip which is located at the top of the slide. The normal position for the jet needle is the *centre* notch. Raising or lowering the needle enriches or weakens the mixture respectively.

Next take the float chamber R off the carburettor. Remove the jet plug Q from the base of the mixing chamber A. Be careful not to lose the two fibre washers (one above and one below the chamber lug). Unscrew the lock-screw X and turn the float chamber cap W until this can be removed from the float chamber. To remove the float itself, compress the spring clip V and withdraw the float T from the float chamber. On removing the plug from the bottom of the float chamber, the needle U will come away. Take care not to mislay the two fibre washers (one above and one below the float-chamber union, *see* Fig. 27).

Now remove the needle-jet O, thereby exposing the main jet P. Afterwards remove the main jet from the needle-jet. Finally unscrew the mixing chamber union nut E and detach the jet block F. Should this be stiff, tap it out gently, using a wooden stump inside the mixing chamber.

Stripping Down Carburettor (1955 Onwards). To remove the "monobloc" carburettor for dismantling and cleaning, first turn off both petrol taps and disconnect the fuel pipe from the float-chamber union. Remove both nuts securing the carburettor flange to the cylinder head and unscrew the knurled cap on top of the mixing chamber. The air and throttle slides can be withdrawn, during or after detaching the carburettor. Do not remove the carburettor slides unless cable or slide renewal is called for.

Referring to Figs. 30–2, dismantling the carburettor is very straightforward. To remove the jet needle 6, withdraw the jet-needle clip 4 on top of the throttle valve 5.

To obtain access to the float 27, remove the three screws 28 securing the cover to the float chamber. Lift out the hinged float 27 and withdraw the moulded-nylon needle 26. Lay both aside for cleaning.

The float-chamber vent is incorporated in the tickler 21, and the top-feed union houses a filter element of fine gauze which is readily accessible for cleaning. To remove the filter gauze, unscrew the banjo bolt 22, remove the banjo 23, and also the gauze.

To remove the main jet 13, remove the main-jet cover 12 and unscrew the jet from the jet holder 14. Remove the jet block locating screw to the left of and slightly below the pilot-air adjusting screw 29. Then push or

THE AMAL CARBURETTOR

tap out the jet block 16 through the larger end of the mixing chamber body. To remove the pilot jet it is only necessary to remove the pilot-jet cover nut 11 and unscrew the jet.

Cleaning. Wash all components thoroughly clean with petrol. Pay special attention to the float chamber, and see that any impurities collected inside are removed completely. Clean the gauze filter occasionally ("monobloc" carburettor), and blow all ducts clear.

Inspection. If the carburettor has been in continuous service for a considerable period, inspect the following—

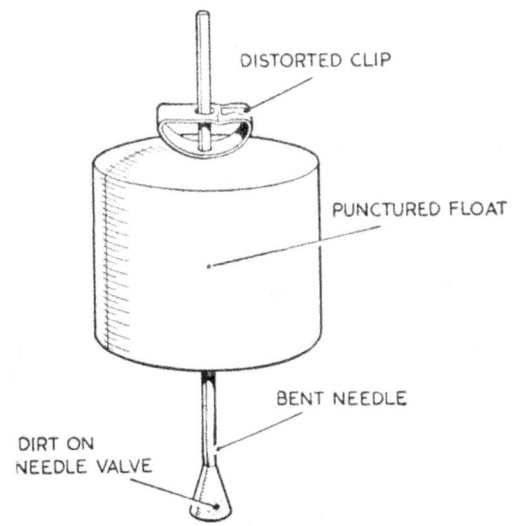

FIG. 35. POSSIBLE CAUSES OF PERSISTENT "FLOODING"
This type of float is fitted to 1938–54 carburettors.

1. FLOAT CHAMBER. Scrutinize the components closely. Hand polish the valve part of the float needle (1938–54 models) by rotating the needle in its seat while pulling it vertically upwards. If a distinct shoulder is visible on the needle where it seats, renew the needle immediately. Examine the needle for signs of bending.

In the case of the "monobloc" carburettor, check that the joint faces of the float-chamber cover and float chamber are not bruised or damaged, and that the joint washer is sound, otherwise it will be difficult to obtain a petrol-tight joint. See that the filter is undamaged.

2. THROTTLE VALVE. Test in the mixing chamber, and if excessive play is present it is advisable to renew the valve without delay.

3. THROTTLE NEEDLE CLIP. This part must securely grip the needle.

Free rotation must *not* take place, otherwise the needle groove will become worn and necessitate a new part being fitted. Be sure to refit the clip in the correct groove.

4. JET BLOCK. If trouble has been experienced with erratic "idling," ascertain by blowing that the pilot jet is clear, and that the pilot outlet in the mixing chamber is unobstructed.

5. CARBURETTOR FLANGE (1955–6). Occasionally check the flange face of the "monobloc" carburettor for truth. Slight distortion sometimes occurs after a considerable mileage. The remedy is to file and rub down the face on emery cloth laid on a surface plate, until a straight-edge shows the face surface to be dead flat. Better still, grind the face.

To Reassemble 1938–54 Carburettor. Referring to Fig. 27, screw the needle-jet O into the jet block F. Now screw the main jet P into the end of the needle-jet. Fit the jet block into the mixing chamber A of the carburettor. It is located by means of a groove and a pin. Then fit the fibre washer and union nut E, and tighten with a fixed spanner.

Position the float T in the float chamber R and then slip the needle U through the bottom of the float chamber and the middle of the float. Compress the spring clip V above the float and pass the needle through the clip also. Then release the spring clip and allow the clip to engage the needle groove. Screw on the float-chamber cap W and secure it by tightening the lock-screw X.

Next attach the float chamber to the mixing chamber of the carburettor. Be sure that you replace the *two* fibre washers, one above and one below the float chamber lug. Then secure the float chamber to the mixing chamber by tightening the jet plug Q. Also fit the plug which secures the petrol pipe union to the base of the float chamber. Here again do not forget the *two* fibre washers.

If removed, fit jet needle C to the throttle valve B so that the needle is in the *middle* position. Then thread the two control cables G, $G1$, through the mixing chamber. The throttle cable G must be nearest to the engine. It can be readily identified, as it has a shorter length of cable protruding from the casing than is the case with the air-control cable.

Slip the two return springs over the control cables. See that the larger spring is placed over the throttle cable. Now fit the air valve D to cable $G1$ and the throttle valve B to cable G. Afterwards fit the air slide to the throttle slide. Then allow both slides to enter the mixing chamber A. Be very careful to see that the jet needle C enters the needle-jet O without any force being used. The jet needle can readily be bent. Now secure the mixing chamber cap Y to the mixing chamber by means of the lock-ring Z which is held after tightening, by the clip $Z1$. Finally secure the carburettor to the induction stub by tightening the clip screw. See that the carburettor is truly vertical, and then reconnect the petrol pipe to the float chamber union.

To Reassemble Carburettor (1955 Onwards). Assemble the instrument in the reverse order of dismantling. Note the following items (*see* Figs. 30, 31). Verify that the washer fitted to the bottom of the jet block 16 is in sound condition. Check the condition also of the washer fitted to the main-jet holder 14, and renew the washer if not perfect. When replacing the throttle valve 5, make sure that the tapered jet-needle does actually enter the hole in the centre of the jet block. Check that the throttle slide moves freely when the mixing-chamber cap 2 is screwed down firmly and held by the retaining spring 18.

When replacing the float 27 in the float chamber, see that the narrower side of the hinge is *uppermost*. Be sure that the joint faces of the float chamber and cover are clean and undamaged. This is important, otherwise petrol leakage may occur. See that the petrol-filter gauze is sound and quite clean (*see* page 54). Before replacing the banjo 23, turn on the petrol tap for a second and observe that petrol flows freely. Make certain that both the nuts securing the carburettor flange to the light-alloy cylinder head are tightened *evenly* and firmly. Avoid using a large spanner for final tightening. The washer at this joint must be perfectly sound. A thick washer should not be used.

To Dismantle Twist-grip and Air Lever. *See* page 103.

CHAPTER V

GENERAL MAINTENANCE

ALL essential instructions are included in this chapter for the routine maintenance, dismantling and assembling of 1938-56 S.V. and O.H.V. Nortons. All Norton engines were substantially redesigned for 1948 onwards. In 1950 a new gearbox was introduced. 1953 saw the advent of "swinging arm" rear suspension, and in 1955 S.V. engines were dropped, and light-alloy heads fitted to all O.H.V. singles.

In this chapter most of the S.V. and O.H.V. maintenance instructions are clearly dated, but note that *where no dating is given, the instructions concerned apply to* 1938 *onwards*.

Norton Spares. When ordering spare parts always remember to quote the type of machine, its year of manufacture, and Engine No. or Frame No. (*see* below). Spares can be obtained from any of the numerous Norton spares stockists.

Large firms (some having many branches) handling general tools, accessories, clothing, etc., include: The Halford Cycle Co., Ltd.; Marble Arch Motor Supplies, Ltd.; Turner's Stores; George Grose, Ltd.; Pride & Clarke, Ltd.; Whitbys of Acton, Ltd.; Claude Rye, Ltd.; E.S. Motors; and James Grose, Ltd.

The Engine and Frame Numbers. You will find the engine number of your mount on the *transmission side of the crankcase*. The frame number is stamped on *the head lug of the frame*, below the steering damper anchor-plate.

TOOLS, ETC.

Items Needed for Maintenance. Items which you must have for the *engine* include: a tin of suitable engine oil (*see* page 33), a drip-tray, a suitable receptacle for draining oil from the oil tank and crankcase, a can of paraffin for cleaning purposes, a stiff brush for scouring dirt from the under side of the engine, some non-fluffy rags, some dishes and jars in which to wash components, a tin of medium-grade valve grinding paste, such as Richford's, some fine emery cloth, some wood or metal boxes in which to store parts pending assembly, a rubber suction-type (or a metal type) valve holder (for O.H.V. engines), a valve spring compressor (*see* page 81), a pair of gudgeon-pin circlips, a set of engine gaskets, some insulation tape, a small wire brush and a good set of feeler gauges for checking the valve clearances (S.V. engines) and plug gap, and a plug regapping tool (*see* Fig. 39).

For the maintenance of the *motor-cycle* parts you will need: a canister of suitable grease (*see* page 38), an oil-can, a small funnel for topping-up the gearbox, a good tyre repair outfit, a tyre pressure gauge (*see* page 4),

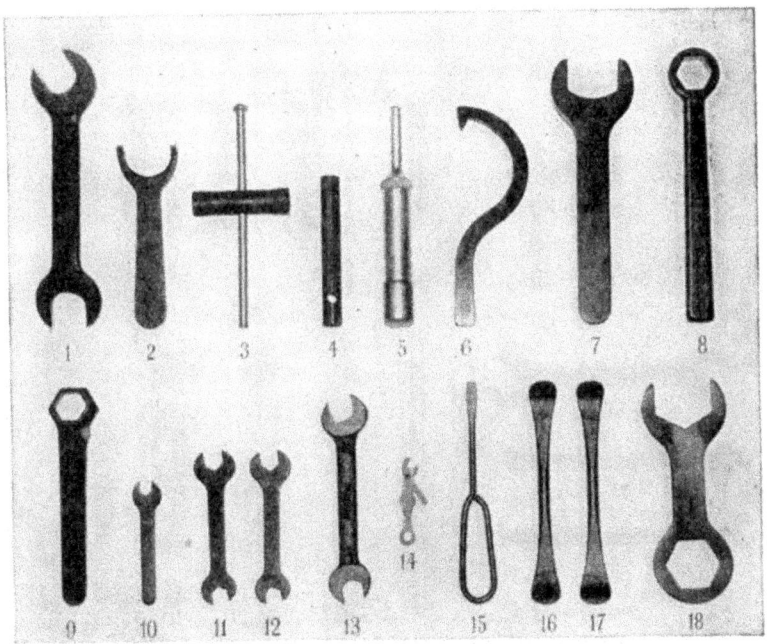

FIG. 36. NORTON TOOL-KIT FOR 1948–53 O.H.V. MODELS

1. Spanner for gearbox top nut.
2. Spanner for locking main-tube top bush of front forks.
3. Double-ended box spanner ($\frac{7}{16}$ in. and $\frac{1}{4}$ in.) and tommy bar.
4. Box spanner for removing wheel nuts (quickly-detachable wheel).
5. Grease-gun for motor-cycle parts.
6. "C" spanner for exhaust-pipe ring nut.
7. Spanner for steering-head adjuster lock-nut.
8. Spanner for hub spindle.
9. Spanner for sparking plug.
10. Single-ended $\frac{1}{2}$ in. spanner.
11. Push-rod adjusting spanner.
12. Push-rod adjusting spanner.
13. Double-ended fixed spanner ($\frac{7}{16}$ in. and $\frac{3}{8}$ in.).
14. "Magdyno" contact-breaker spanner and gauge.
15. Screwdriver.
16. Tyre lever.
17. Tyre lever.
18. Spanner for front-fork filler plugs and steering head adjuster-nut.

a box of spare chain links, a chain rivet extractor (*see* page 61), a bottle containing distilled water, a Lucas battery filler (a hydrometer is also desirable), a sponge and pail (where no hose is available), a chamois leather, some soft dusters, some rags (old shirts will do), some good polish for the enamelled parts, and last, but by no means least, some good hands cleanser. If you are an all-weather rider, it is advisable to obtain some cleaning compound (such as "Gunk") for the machine.

The Norton Tool-kit. The kit supplied with each brand new Norton should be sufficient for all normal stripping down and maintenance work.

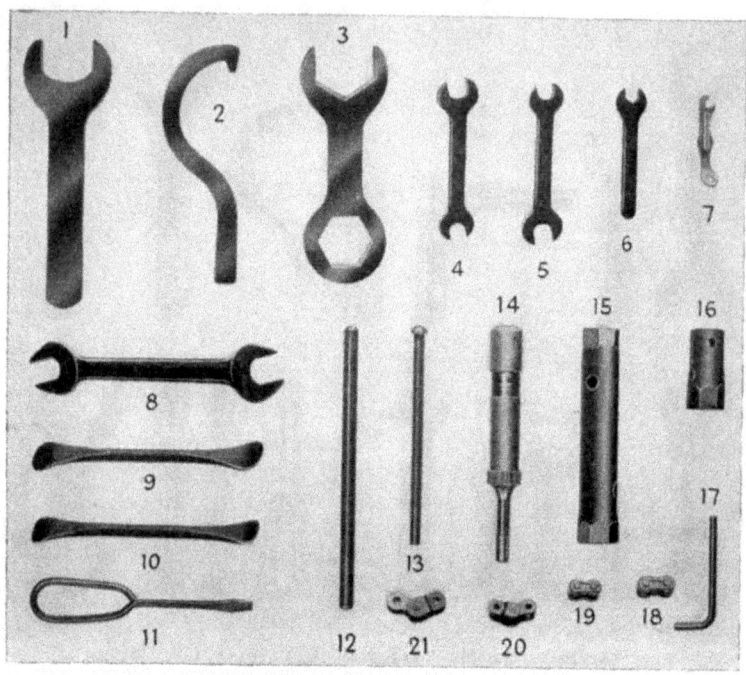

FIG. 36A. NORTON TOOL-KIT FOR 1954 AND LATER O.H.V. MODELS

1. Spanner for steering-head adjuster lock-nut.
2. "C" spanner for exhaust-pipe ring nut.
3. Spanner for front-fork filler plugs and steering-head adjuster nut.
4, 5. Push-rod adjusting spanners ($\frac{1}{4}$ in. and $\frac{5}{16}$ in. B.S.F.).
6. Spanner ($\frac{1}{4}$ in.) for control cable adjusters.
7. "Magdyno" contact-breaker spanner and gauge.
8. Fixed spanner ($\frac{7}{16}$ in. and $\frac{3}{8}$ in. B.S.F.) for general use.
9, 10. Tyre levers.
11. Screwdriver.
12, 13. Tommy bars.
14. Grease-gun for motor-cycle parts.
15. Box spanner for rear-wheel spindle nuts.
16. Box spanner for sparking plug.
17. Handlebar clamp key.
18–21. Spare chain links.

It includes essential tools and a grease-gun for greasing motor-cycle parts. The standard tool-kit for 1948–56 O.H.V. models (18, 19R, 19S, ES2, 50) is shown in Figs. 36 and 36A.

GENERAL MAINTENANCE

The tool-kit supplied for 1948–54 S.V. Models 16H and 1 is identical with that in Fig. 36 except that a pair of tappet spanners is substituted for the push-rod adjusting spanners shown at 11 and 12, a cylinder-head securing nut spanner is included, and the sparking plug spanner 9 is modified to suit the rather deep finning of the light-alloy head.

The standard Norton tool-kit for S.V. and O.H.V. models does not include an adjustable spanner, nor a pair of pliers. The former is useful and a small pair of snipe-nose pliers is *necessary* when removing a gudgeon-pin circlip in order to remove the piston from the connecting-rod.

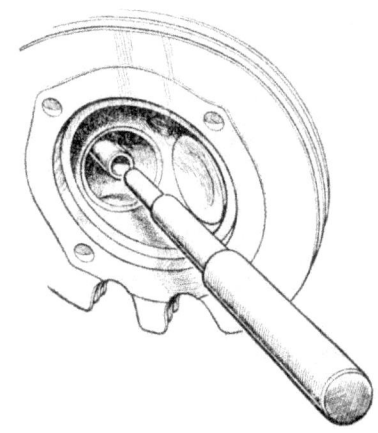

FIG. 37. A USEFUL DRIFT FOR REMOVING AND FITTING NORTON VALVE GUIDES

A good 6 in. adjustable spanner (Part No. A2/564) and a 6 in. pair of pliers (Part No. A2/572) are obtainable from Norton spares stockists for 7s. and 5s. respectively.* Two other Norton tools which it is desirable to obtain are a pull-through (Part No. B2/685) for the telescopic front forks, and a chain rivet extractor (Part No. A2/569). These two tools are priced at 7s. 6d. and 5s. 6d. respectively.* In all cases postage is extra.

Two Excellent Proprietary Tools. Messrs. Taylor Matterson, Ltd., who handle spares, can supply two tools which may interest Norton owners who overhaul their machines. One tool is a valve-guide drift, and the other an extractor for withdrawing the clutch centre. The firm's address is 81-3 Bedford Hill, Balham, S.W.12.

Fig. 37 shows the "T.M." valve-guide drift which closely fits inside the valve guide and ensures that the guide is driven out or fitted *squarely*. It is

---

* All prices quoted are, of course, subject to alteration without notice by the manufacturers.

cadmium plated and is obtainable in two sizes. A good feature of the tool is the length of the handle which enables the drift to be held firmly and comfortably when directing hammer blows on it.

Fig. 38 illustrates the "T.M." extractor for removing the clutch centre which fits tightly on the gearbox mainshaft splines. To remove a tightly-fitted clutch centre, screw the body of the extractor into the large threaded hole in the clutch centre and then turn the tommy bar until the clutch centre is withdrawn from the gearbox mainshaft.

Cleaning the Chromium. Never employ liquid metal polish or paste, as this will wear down the thin surface. A good chromium-cleaning compound can, however, safely be used. The normal method of removing

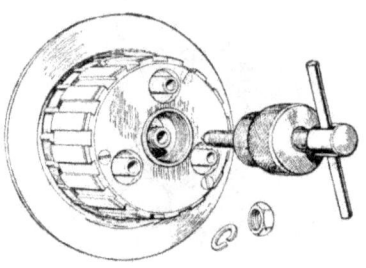

FIG. 38. A HANDY EXTRACTOR FOR REMOVING THE CLUTCH CENTRE

tarnish (salt deposits) is to clean the surfaces regularly with a damp chamois leather and then polish them with soft dusters.

To Reduce Tarnishing. During the winter months it is a good plan to wipe over occasionally all surfaces with a soft cloth soaked in a proprietary anti-tarnish preparation. An example is "Tekall," obtainable in ½ pint and 1 pint tins.

Cleaning the Engine and Gearbox. See that the cylinder barrel and cylinder-head fins are kept clean and black (except alloy heads). If the enamel has worn away, paint the fins with some proprietary cylinder black after thorough cleaning with a stiff brush dipped in paraffin. Note that rusted fins, besides looking shabby, cause an appreciable loss in heat dispersion.

Scour off all filth from the lower part of the engine and gearbox with stiff brushes and paraffin. Clean all aluminium alloy and bright surfaces with a rag damped in paraffin, assisted by brushes where necessary.

To Clean the Enamel. Never attempt to remove mud from the enamelled parts when dry and caked, as this is likely to damage the surfaces. Soak the mud off with a hose if available. In the case of a very dirty machine it

GENERAL MAINTENANCE

may be advisable to paint the surfaces over with a cleaning compound such as "Gunk" before directing a stream of water on to the dirty surfaces. Be careful not to allow any water to get inside vulnerable parts such as the "Magdyno" and carburettor. If a hose is not available, soak the mud and then disperse it with plenty of clean water, using a sponge and pail.

Having removed all dirt, dry the enamelled surfaces with a chamois leather and afterwards polish them with soft dusters and some good wax polish or a proprietary polish such as "Karpol."

"Dry weather" riders can keep a machine in almost showroom condition merely by rubbing the enamel over with a paraffin-damped rag, followed by a dry, soft duster.

Run-in a New Engine Carefully. Go very steady during the first 1,000 miles and put into practice the important advice given on page 9. Avoid large throttle openings and make full use of the gearbox.

Check Nuts for Tightness. This is particularly important during running-in (*see* page 9), as some "bedding down" of parts occurs. Regularly apply spanners to the various external nuts to ensure tightness, paying special attention to the engine bolts and nuts, the engine mounting nuts, and the pipe unions. After running-in, make a regular check once a month, but after decarbonizing and running for a short mileage, check the cylinder-head nuts for tightness.

Obtaining Good Carburation. For hints on setting the controls for easy starting, *see* page 5. Chapter IV tells you how the Amal carburettor works and how to tune and clean it.

Correct Lubrication. For detailed instructions, see Chapter III. A lubrication chart is given on page 37.

Care of Lighting Equipment. For instructions concerning the dynamo portion of the Lucas "Magdyno," the lamps, battery, and horn, refer to Chapter II. Wiring diagrams will be found on pages 27–29.

THE IGNITION SYSTEM

This section deals with the all-important sparking plug, and the ignition components of the Lucas "Magdyno." Ignition timing is covered in the section on page 96.

Suitable Sparking Plugs. For the appropriate Lodge, K.L.G., and Champion plug recommendations *see* pages 9–10.

Sparking Plug Gap. Difficult starting or occasional misfiring can usually be traced to a dirty or defective sparking plug. The life of a good plug is considerable, but the points of the electrodes gradually burn away and eventually the gap becomes enlarged considerably, and it is necessary to reset the points.

It is advisable to check the plug gap regularly (say every 2,000 miles) and to adjust the gap if burning of the points has caused the gap to exceed 0·022 in. Norton Motors, Ltd. recommend a gap of 0·018–0·022 in. For obvious reasons, when re-gapping it is advisable to set the gap at or near the *bottom* limit. Check the gap with a wire or feeler gauge. The gauge should just enter without springing the points.

When adjusting the plug gap, never attempt to bend or tap the centre electrode. Use a pair of snipe-nose pliers, or a plug regapping tool (shown

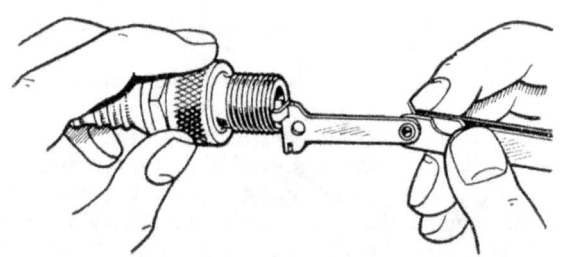

FIG. 39. A SAFE METHOD OF RE-GAPPING A PLUG
The Champion tool shown includes suitable gauges

in Fig. 39), to bend the outside (earth) electrode. Tapping the earth electrode is not a good method. When the plug has to be thoroughly cleaned, this should be done as described below, and the plug re-gapped *afterwards*.

Cleaning the Plug. If carburation is correct and excessive oil is not entering the combustion chamber, it should not be necessary to dismantle and clean the sparking plug thoroughly more often than once about every 3,000 miles. When running-in a new or rebored engine, it is advisable to remove and check the plug for cleanliness at intervals of about 500 miles.

Quick cleaning of a plug can be done by brushing the points and slightly rubbing their firing sides with some smooth emery cloth. Alternatively the plug can be cleaned with a proprietary gadget. Thorough cleaning (internal and external), however, is not possible without dismantling the plug (*see* below).

To Clean Lodge and K.L.G. Plugs Thoroughly. Fig 40 shows a typical detachable type (K.L.G.) sparking plug dismantled for thorough cleaning. To dismantle a detachable-type sparking plug, hold the smaller hexagon of the gland nut *B* lightly in a vice or with a suitable spanner. If you use a vice, be most careful not to exert any pressure on the hexagon faces. Then with a suitable spanner applied to the larger hexagon *E* of the plug body, unscrew the body until it is separated from the gland nut. The centre electrode *F* with its insulation (comprising the insulated electrode assembly *A*) can now be detached from the gland nut. Take care not to lose the internal sealing washer *H*.

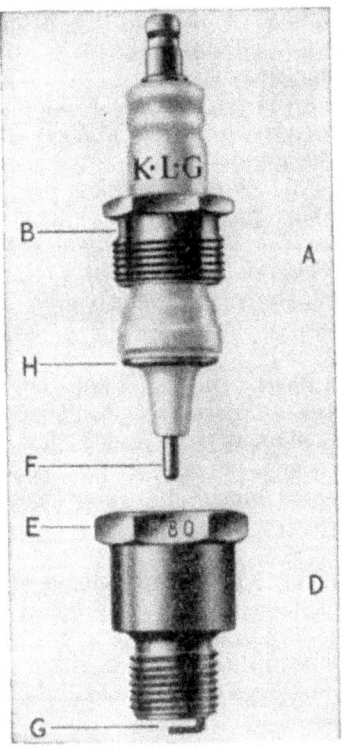

Fig. 40. Detachable Type Sparking Plug (K.L.G.) Dismantled for Thorough Cleaning

The gland nut *B* and the internal washer *H* are shown still in position on the insulation.

To clean the "Sintox" or "Corundite" insulation, used on Lodge and K.L.G. plugs respectively, wipe it clean with a cloth soaked in petrol or paraffin. If the insulation is coated with hard carbon deposits, remove these with some fine emery cloth, but make no attempt to scrape off the deposits. The internal sealing washer *H* and the surfaces on the insulator, and in the metal body on which this washer rests, are very important as they prevent gas leakage through the plug. Therefore wipe them only with a rag soaked in petrol or paraffin. Any damage caused while dismantling will render the plug unserviceable.

To clean the metal parts (plug body and gland nut), wipe them clean with petrol, or, if necessary, scrape off the deposits with a small knife, or use a wire brush. Afterwards rinse the parts in petrol. The gland nut seldom gets very fouled, but the inside of the plug body may be very dirty, and the same may apply to the external threads of the plug. Clean and polish the points of the centre and outside (earth) electrodes F and G (Fig. 40) with some fine emery cloth.

See that there is no dirt or grit lodged between the body of the plug and the insulation, and particularly on the internal sealing washer and the contacting faces. Smear a little thin oil on the internal washer and make sure that it seats properly. When assembling the sparking plug, see that the centre electrode and insulation are positioned centrally in the body bore. If it is not, remove, re-position by rotating the centre a quarter of a turn, and reassemble. Do not attempt to force it into position or bend it.

Avoid excessive tightening of the gland nut B. Finally verify that the plug gap is correct (*see* page 64).

To Clean Champion Plugs. To clean a non-detachable type Champion plug, take it to the nearest garage equipped with a Champion Service Unit. With this apparatus the plug can be cleaned in a few minutes of all deposits, washed, subjected to a high pressure air line, and afterwards tested for sparking on the Champion apparatus at an air pressure of over 100 lb per sq in.

Replacing Sparking Plug. Before replacing a plug, renew the copper washer if it is worn or flattened, and clean the plug threads with a wire brush. Screw the plug home by hand as far as possible, and always use the box spanner in the Norton tool kit for final tightening. An adjustable spanner should not be used, as this may cause distortion.

The "Magdyno" Contact-breaker Gap. Little attention to the ignition portion of the Lucas "Magdyno" is needed, other than occasional lubrication (*see* page 35) and attention to the face-cam type contact-breaker, shown in Fig. 41. Any serious internal trouble should be dealt with by a Lucas service agent.

The contacts of the contact-breaker (Fig. 41) should be examined on a new machine after the first 500 miles, and subsequently about every 2,500 miles. If the "break," with the contacts fully open is appreciably more, or less, than will just hold a 0·010–0·012 in. blade of a feeler gauge the contacts should be adjusted (*after* cleaning, if necessary). Too great a gap will advance the timing. The magneto-spanner gauge (shown at 14 in Fig. 36), or the blade of a proprietary set of feelers, can be useful for checking the "break," the procedure for which is as follows—

GENERAL MAINTENANCE

1. Remove the contact-breaker cover and rotate the engine slowly forwards until the contacts of the contact-breaker are wide open (i.e. near T.D.C. on the compression stroke).
2. Insert the blade of the feeler gauge between the contacts.
3. If the feeler gauge *just* slides in without friction, the gap is correct and no adjustment is needed. If the gauge is a slack fit or the contacts have to be sprung to enable it to enter, adjust the gap as below.
4. With the magneto spanner loosen the lock-nut which secures the adjustable contact screw (*see* Fig. 41) and then adjust this screw by means

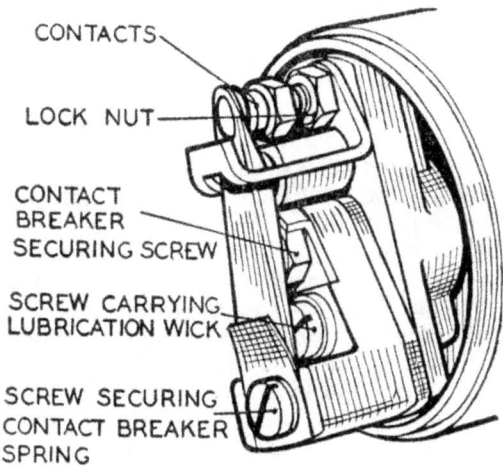

FIG. 41. THE FACE-CAM TYPE CONTACT-BREAKER ON THE LUCAS "MAGDYNO" (1938 ONWARDS)

of its hexagon head until the correct gap is obtained between the fixed and movable contacts.

5. Retighten the contact screw lock-nut and again check the gap. If correct, replace the contact-breaker cover.

Cleaning the "Magdyno" Contacts. At intervals of about 2,500 miles, when checking the contact-breaker gap, scrutinize the contacts closely. If the contacts are allowed to become dirty or oily, rapid burning, pitting, and consequent ignition trouble will ensue.

If inspection reveals that the contacts have a *grey, frosted* appearance, with no blackening or pitting, do not interfere with them (assuming that the gap is correct). If the contacts are only slightly discoloured, clean them with a rag moistened with petrol.

On examination after a big mileage the contacts may be found to have irregular and blackened areas due to pitting and burning (especially if the contacts have not been kept clean and correctly adjusted). In this case it is essential to clean them up, otherwise misfiring and rapid deterioration of the contacts will follow.

To clean the contacts, use a *fine* carborundum slip or a piece of *fine* emery cloth (do not use a nail file), and with the contact-breaker spring arm (*see* Fig. 41) removed, clean and polish the contacts until all pitting disappears and the contact surfaces are smooth all over. Be careful to keep the contact faces "square" as well as uniform. *This is most important.**
If pitting is not appreciable it is permissible to insert the emery cloth between the two contacts, while both are in position. If pitting is serious, and in order to examine the contacts effectively, the spring arm must be removed. Remove any traces of rust from the arm.

To remove the spring arm (carrying the moving contact) on a face-cam type contact-breaker (*see* Fig. 41), it is only necessary to remove its securing screw and spring washer. When replacing the spring arm, make certain that the small backing spring is replaced immediately under the securing screw and spring washer, with the curved portion facing *outwards* as shown in Fig. 41. See that the contacts are perfectly aligned before tightening the securing screw.

Where very deep pitting is present, it may be necessary to remove the complete contact-breaker after detaching the spring arm. To do this, unlock the tab-washer and remove the contact-breaker securing screw, when the complete contact-breaker can be withdrawn, and dealt with on a bench or table if desired. When replacing the contact-breaker, see that a new tab-washer is fitted and locked over the securing screw. It is not advisable to remove much metal from the contacts, and if a reasonable amount of facing up fails to restore the surfaces to normal, fit a new pair of contacts (including, of course, a new spring arm). After dealing with the contacts as described, wipe away any metal dust with a petrol-dampened cloth and check the gap.

The Slip-ring. Moisture, oil, or dirt accumulating on the "Magdyno" slip-ring is liable to cause difficult starting and misfiring. Very occasionally remove the h.t. pick-up from the "Magdyno" and thoroughly clean the flanges and track of the slip-ring. Do this by holding a soft, dry cloth, wrapped round a pencil, through the pick-up hole, and, with the cloth lightly pressed against the slip-ring, slowly turn the engine. The h.t. pick-up is secured to the body of the "Magdyno" by two small screws which must be removed.

The H.T. Pick-up. When cleaning the slip-ring, also clean the surface of the pick-up moulding with a cloth moistened with petrol, and polish with a fine, dry cloth. Examine the pick-up moulding for cracks, and closely

---

* Note that the latest type Lucas contacts have slightly convex (not flat) faces, which must be cleaned with fine emery cloth only.

GENERAL MAINTENANCE

inspect the spring and carbon brush. The brush must move freely in its holder, but be careful not to stretch the spring. Renew the spring at once if it has weakened, and always renew a badly worn brush. When replacing the h.t. pick-up, do not forget to replace the small gasket between the body of the "Magdyno" and the pick-up moulding.

To Renew the H.T. Cable. When renewing a cracked or perished h.t. cable, always use 7 mm rubber-covered ignition cable. Bare the end of the cable (*see* Fig. 42) for about ¼ in. and thread the cable through the moulded

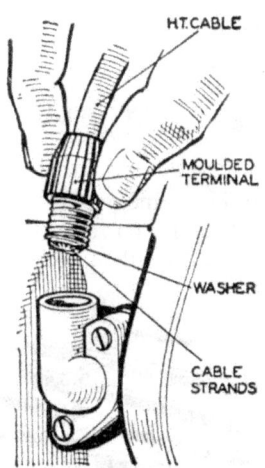

FIG. 42. RENEWING LUCAS H.T. CABLE

terminal nut. Pass the wire through the bronze washer and then bend back the cable strands as illustrated. Finally screw the moulded terminal nut into the pick-up connexion.

The "Magdyno" Chain. Lubrication is quite automatic, the chain being lubricated by the engine (*see* page 33). For chain tension, see page 103.

Removing Lucas "Magdyno" (1938 Onwards). For instructions on removing the "Magdyno," see the appropriate paragraph on page 102.

VALVE CLEARANCES

In order that the inlet and exhaust valves shall seat properly and have the correct degree of lift at normal running temperature, it is extremely important that the correct clearances should exist when the engine is *cold* between the valve stems and the tappet heads, or rocker pads, as the case may be, according to whether the engine be of S.V. or O.H.V. type. The clearances should be checked now and again with a feeler gauge of the right thickness (S.V. engines) or by feeling the push-rods (O.H.V. engines). It is unlikely that adjustment will be needed, unless a big mileage has been completed, or the engine is new, or reconditioned, or the valves have been ground-in.

TABLE IV

VALVE CLEARANCES RECOMMENDED (1938–47)
(ENGINE COLD)

Engine (see page 72)	Inlet Valve	Exhaust Valve
S.V. (1938–47)	0·004 in.	0·006 in.
O.H.V. Push-rod (1938–47) . . .	Nil	Nil

When Checking. Turn the engine over until compression is felt after the inlet valve has just closed, and then raise the exhaust-valve lifter a trifle, and further rotate the engine until the piston is at the top of its stroke and

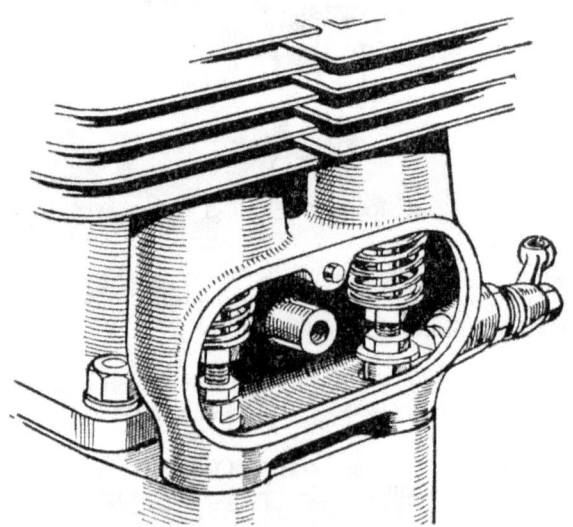

FIG. 43. TAPPET ADJUSTMENT ON S.V. ENGINES
(1938–54)

both valves are closed. See that the exhaust-valve lifter is in no way determining the clearance. There should be an appreciable interval between the moment when the lifter is raised and the exhaust valve is lifted off its seat.

Adjusting Valve Clearances (1938–54 S.V., 1938–56 O.H.V.). The correct valve clearances for 1938–56 engines are given in Tables IV, V. The adjustment is illustrated in Figs. 43–45. All the necessary adjustments must be made with the engine *cold*, and it is important first to verify

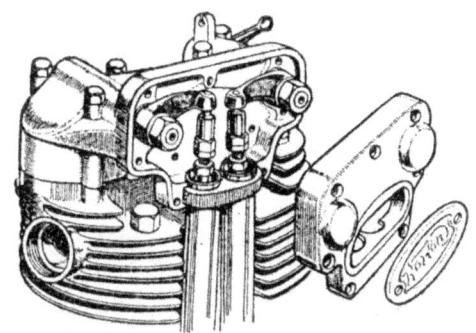

FIG. 44. PUSH-ROD ADJUSTMENT ON O.H.V. ENGINES (1938–47)

(*By courtesy of "The Motor Cycle," London*)

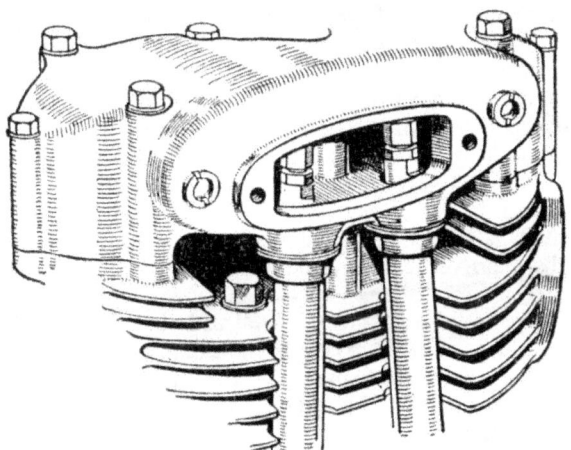

FIG. 45. PUSH-ROD ADJUSTMENT ON O.H.V. ENGINES (1948 ONWARDS)

that the exhaust valve lifter is quite clear of the exhaust valve when the piston is at T.D.C. on the compression stroke. On O.H.V. engines a clearance of *nil* implies that the push-rods must be just free to rotate without any up-and-down movement.

To make a valve clearance adjustment on a 1938–54 S.V. or 1938–56 O.H.V. Norton engine, loosen the middle hexagon (lock-nut) by holding with one spanner the bottom hexagon or flats (1948–56) on the tappet stem or push-rod, and applying a spanner to the middle hexagon. Then turn the top hexagon of the tappet head or push-rod adjuster as required to obtain the correct valve clearance. Tighten the middle hexagon (lock-nut) and again check the clearance. Deal with both tappets or push-rods similarly.

TABLE V

VALVE CLEARANCES RECOMMENDED (1948 ONWARDS)
(ENGINE COLD)

Engine Valve	Model 16H	Model 1*	Models 18, 19R, 19S, ES2, 50
Inlet	0·002 in.	0·002 in.	None
Exhaust	0·003 in.	0·003 in.	None

Where Engine Number has Suffix "Q." Special care must be taken when adjusting the valve clearances of all S.V. and O.H.V. engines which have the engine number followed by the letter "Q." The reason for this is that such engines have a modified cam-form requiring a different procedure, which is as follows—

To adjust the clearance for the inlet valve, turn the engine until the exhaust valve is just lifting. Then adjust the inlet tappet or push-rod as described. Similarly, to adjust the exhaust valve clearance, turn the engine until the inlet valve has just closed, and proceed to make the required adjustment. The correct valve clearance for S.V. engines is 0·010 in. for both valves. On O.H.V. engines both push-rods should be just free to rotate, but have no vertical movement.

Exhaust Valve Lifter Adjustment. As already mentioned, it is important that there should be some backlash at the exhaust-valve lifter lever, for it would inevitably prevent the exhaust valve from seating properly, and thus cause loss of compression and burning of the valve and its seating, accompanied by intermittent banging in the exhaust pipe and silencer.

There should be sufficient backlash in the control cable to ensure that the exhaust valve lifter cam is always kept well clear of the exhaust-tappet collar (S.V.), or the rocker arm (O.H.V.) inside the rocker-box, when the valve lifter is not in use. The desired adjustment may be effected by means of the adjustable cable-stop placed, in the case of the S.V. engine, close to the exhaust port, and on the near side of the rocker-box on the O.H.V.

* Model 1 is more generally referred to as the Big 4.

engines. If necessary, you can adjust the position of the operating arm to which the "business end" of the cable is attached.

DECARBONIZING ENGINE

After 5,000–8,000 miles have been covered, the accumulation of carbon deposits on the piston crown and in various parts of the combustion chamber results in the engine losing its original "kick," and there is a marked decline in general all-round performance, accompanied by a tendency for knocking under the slightest provocation. In addition, the exhaust note becomes "woolly," and loses its virile crispness and low boom. When this happens it is a sure indication that the time has come for undertaking a "top overhaul," or, in other words, for decarbonizing and perhaps grinding-in the valves.

When decarbonizing your Norton it is always worth while inspecting the valve seatings and, *if necessary*, grinding-in the valves. Removal of the valves incidentally facilitates thorough cleaning of the ports.

The S.V. Engines. The S.V. type is perhaps the easiest to decarbonize, and involves simply the removal of the detachable cylinder head, unless it is desired to remove the piston when the cylinder barrel must also be removed complete with valves (although, if preferred, these may be removed first), after first removing the protective aluminium cover. Removal of the cylinder barrel is not advised too often.

The Overhead-valve Engines. All Norton O.H.V. engines have detachable cylinder heads, and it is unnecessary to detach the cylinder barrel unless it is desired to remove the piston, to inspect it and also the piston rings. In order to remove the cylinder head, however, it is necessary first to detach the push-rods complete with covers, and also the rocker-box. On 1955 and later engines the head and rocker-box must be removed *together*.

Initial Preparations. Jack the machine upon its stand and get out the tool-kit. If the engine exterior is very dirty, go over it with a rag damped in paraffin, taking special care to clean the parts about to be dismantled, and see that a clean box or other receptacle is at hand in which to place the various parts prior to reassembly. Put the engine on compression and begin stripping the machine of those parts which obstruct easy removal of the cylinder head.

DECARBONIZING 1938–47 MODELS

Removing and Fitting Petrol Tank. Petrol tank removal is advised when decarbonizing all models, with the exception of a top overhaul of a S.V. machine involving cylinder head removal only.

Draining is unnecessary, but verify that the petrol taps are both turned to the "Off" position. In this position the round end of each tap is pressed in. Disconnect the fuel pipes from the taps, gripping the union nut with one spanner and applying a second one to the tap union. To free the petrol tank from the frame on 1938 and later models, remove the four securing bolts and washers. Two steel washers and two rubber washers will be found at each tank support (*see* Fig. 46).

To replace the petrol tank, lay the four shouldered rubber washers on the frame tank brackets, and place the four steel washers above them.

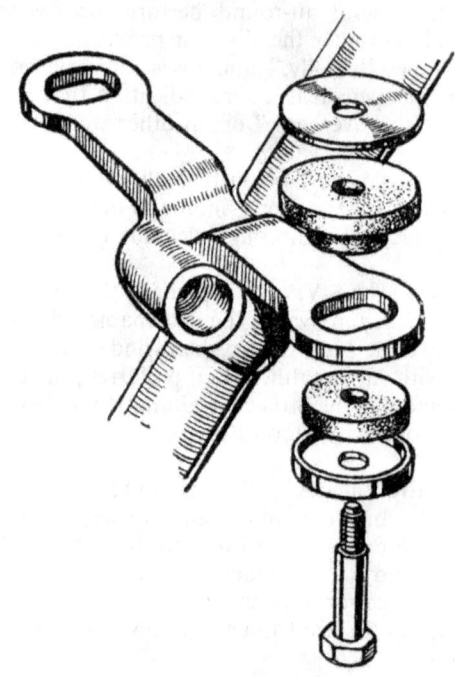

Fig. 46. Correct Order for Assembling Fuel Tank Mounting Washers (1938 Onwards)

Then position the petrol tank and fit the four cupped steel and the four rubber washers on to the tank securing bolts. The correct order of assembling the washers is clearly illustrated in Fig. 46. Next fit the four bolts to the tank and tighten them evenly. Verify that the tank does not at any point foul the frame, and finally replace the petrol pipes, using two spanners as for dismantling.

Removing the S.V. Cylinder Head (1938–47). Remove the h.t. lead from the sparking plug and the plug also. Then remove the nine nuts which secure the cylinder head to the barrel, and lift off the cylinder head and the joint washer.

GENERAL MAINTENANCE

Decarbonizing S.V. Models (1938–47). When undertaking a top overhaul of a Model 16H or "Big Four," scrape off all carbon from the top of the piston (*see* page 79) and inside of the cylinder head, being careful not to damage the piston, which is of a light-alloy. It is not advisable to remove *all* carbon from the edge of the piston crown, as this carbon forms an effective oil seal and prevents excessive oil consumption (*see* page 92).

Replacing the S.V. Cylinder Head (1938–47). Inspect the joint washer and renew it if there is evidence of blowing. Fit this washer with its bright

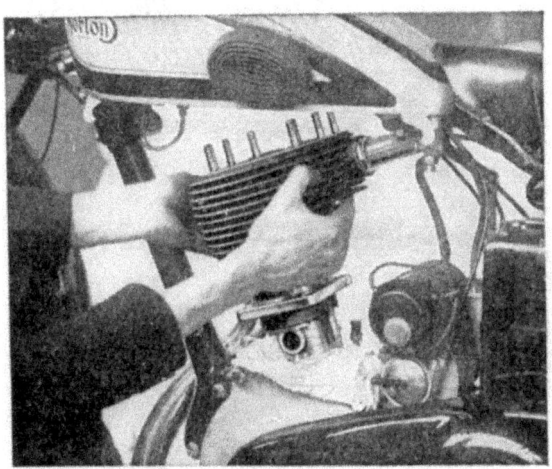

FIG. 47. REMOVING CYLINDER BARREL (S.V.)
The barrel must be lifted off vertically on 1938–47 O.H.V. models. Be careful not to move it sideways as this may bend the connecting-rod. Also block up the crankcase mouth with a rag when removing the barrel.

side *towards* the cylinder barrel. Replace the cylinder head and tighten down the nine nuts evenly. Finally replace the sparking plug and h.t. lead.

Removing the S.V. Cylinder Barrel, etc. (1938–47). It is possible to remove a Model 16H or "Big Four" cylinder barrel with or without the cylinder head in position. But first remove the petrol tank (*see* page 73) and detach the h.t. lead and sparking plug. Next remove the Amal carburettor, complete with petrol pipes, from the induction stub. Loosen the bolt on the split ring and ease off the carburettor, allowing it to be suspended from the throttle and air control cables.

Remove the cover from the valve chest and turn the engine over until the piston is at B.D.C. with both valves closed. Detach the exhaust-valve lifter control from the arm (*see* Fig. 43) by lifting the arm and releasing the

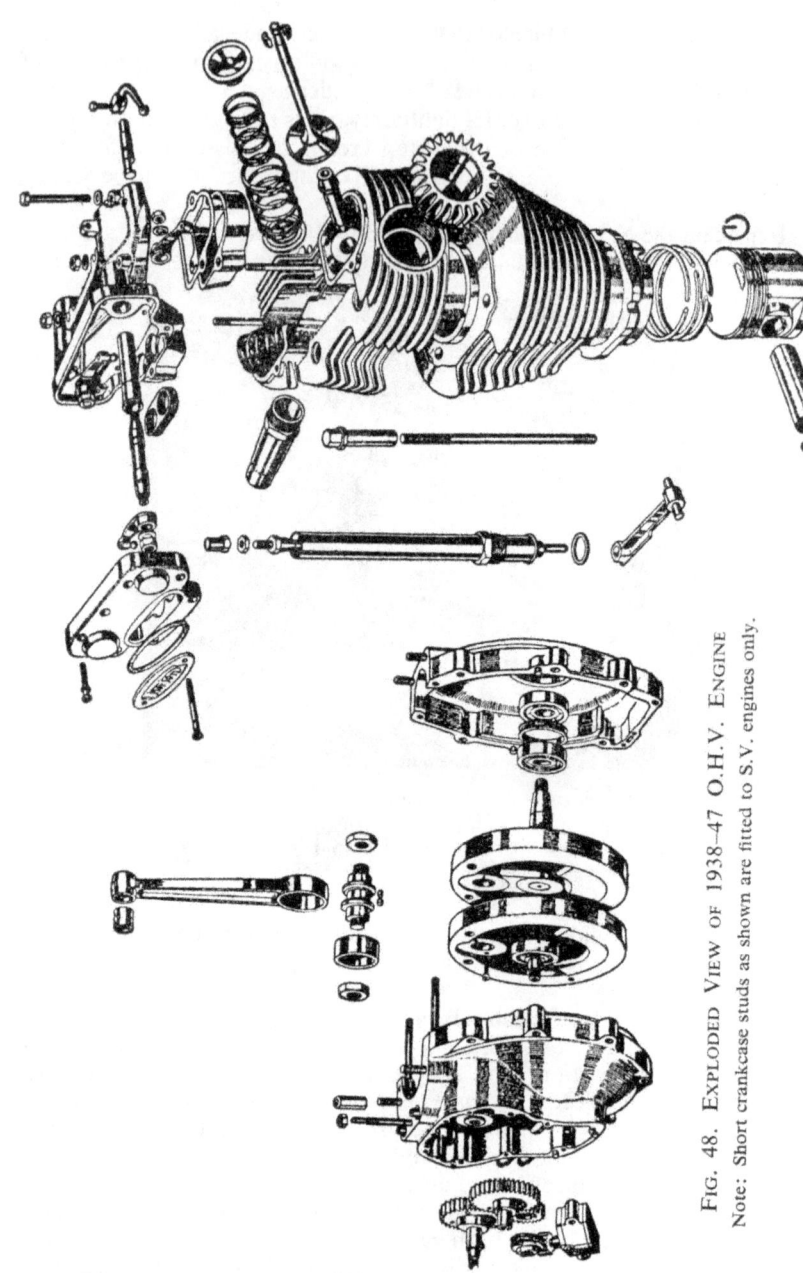

Fig. 48. Exploded View of 1938–47 O.H.V. Engine
Note: Short crankcase studs as shown are fitted to S.V. engines only.

inner cable. This will free the return spring, and the cable adjuster can be unscrewed from the cylinder barrel, rendering the cable completely disconnected. Now remove from the cylinder barrel the exhaust-valve lifter spindle, which is secured by a set-pin in the base of the cylinder. Take out this set-pin and remove the spindle, complete with oil-retaining washer and spring.

To free the cylinder barrel, remove the five nuts from the studs at its base. One of these nuts will be found *inside* the valve chest. Now carefully withdraw the cylinder barrel in the manner shown in Fig. 47. It should be noted that a paper washer is interposed between the crankcase and the cylinder barrel; also that it is not necessary to remove the valve guide lubricator (where provided). Cover up the mouth of the crankcase with a large clean cloth to prevent any foreign matter entering the crankcase. Then proceed with piston removal, To do this, remove *one* circlip and push out the gudgeon-pin, which is a running fit in the small-end bush. Mark the piston to ensure correct replacement, and scrap the circlip which has been removed.

Removing O.H.V. Rocker-box, Cylinder Head, Cylinder Barrel, etc. (1938-47). First remove the petrol tank (*see* page 73). Also remove the Amal carburettor, with petrol pipes, from the induction stub, after first loosening the clip-securing screw. Take off the exhaust pipe, or detach the complete exhaust system as a unit.

Turn the engine over until both valves are closed, and remove the sparking plug and rocker-adjustment inspection cover. Next remove the rocker-box cover, the rocker-box securing bolts and nuts, the rocker-box itself, and the two distance pieces. These and other components are clearly shown in Fig. 48, which shows an exploded view of the 1938-47 O.H.V. engine.

Detach both push-rods and cover tubes, being careful not to mix up the inlet and exhaust members. Unscrew the four cylinder-head nuts, leaving the rocker-box hanging from the exhaust-valve lifter cable, or, alternatively, remove completely. Withdraw the cylinder head from the cylinder barrel spigot. The cylinder barrel itself should not be removed each time the engine is decarbonized, as the top of the piston can be scraped clean as on the S.V. models (*see* page 75).

If it is desired to remove the cylinder barrel also in order to examine the piston and piston rings, turn the engine over until the piston is at B.D.C. and lift the barrel off vertically (*see* Fig. 47), while supporting the piston with the hand. Cover up the mouth of the crankcase with a cloth, and proceed to remove the piston. Take out both gudgeon-pin circlips (*see* page 91) and then push out the gudgeon-pin. If stiff, tap the pin out while supporting the piston firmly on the opposite side; better still, press out the gudgeon-pin with a proprietary gudgeon-pin removal tool. Scratch a nick on the end of the gudgeon-pin and an "F" (front) mark on the inside of the piston to ensire correct replacement, which is essential. Decarbonize thoroughly (*see* page 79). If it is decided not to fit new piston rings, it is best not to disturb the carbon which has probably formed at the backs of the rings. The removal and inspection of piston rings are dealt with below. Valve grinding is dealt with on page 81.

Examining and Removing Piston Rings. The piston rings are the mainguard of the compression. They must, therefore, be full of spring, free in their grooves, and set with their slots opposite to each other (i.e. at 120° in the case of the three-ring piston which is fitted on all type Norton engines).

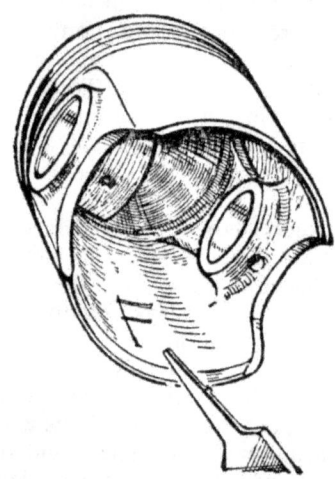

FIG. 49. MARKING INSIDE OF PISTON TO ENSURE CORRECT REPLACEMENT
(*By courtesy of* "*The Motor-Cycle,*" *London*)

If all three rings are bright all the way round, they are obviously being polished against the cylinder walls, and are perfect, and should be left alone. If, on the other hand, they are dull or stained at some points, they are not in proper contact with the walls of the cylinder. Perhaps they are stuck in their grooves with burnt oil, and will function properly if the grooves are cleaned. If vertically loose in their grooves or very badly marked, the rings must be renewed. Piston rings are of cast-iron and, being of very small section, must be handled very, very carefully. If not, they will certainly be broken. They cannot safely be opened out wider than will allow them to slip over the crown of the piston. Therefore, to put them on or remove them requires the insertion of small strips of metal, about $\frac{1}{2}$ in. wide by 2 in. long, which are placed in the manner illustrated by Fig. 50. Be most careful to note the order in which the rings are removed so as to ensure proper replacement.

GENERAL MAINTENANCE

When fitting any *new* rings,* thoroughly clean the grooves into which they fit, as any deposit left at the back will force new rings out and make them too tight a fit. Paraffin usually loosens stuck piston rings. Piston rings are made to very accurate dimensions, and it is very bad practice to attempt to "fit" oversize or undersize rings unless you know exactly what you are doing. Lapping-in oversize piston rings is a skilful job, and unless the slot sizes are exactly right, the rings will not function well, and may even produce an engine "seizure." Therefore, always use piston rings

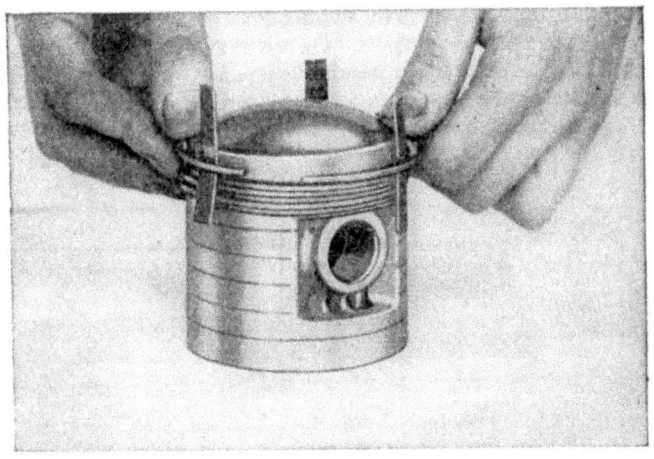

Fig. 50. A Safe Method of Removing and Fitting Piston Rings

supplied by Norton Motors, Ltd. The correct gap at the slots for all 1938–47 plain rings is 0·015–0·020 in. and for the oil control rings 0·008 in. For side clearance of the rings in their grooves, *see* page 83.

Removing the Carbon. Thoroughness in decarbonizing well repays the labour expended. To clean the cylinder head, the best tool is a blunt knife or screwdriver, or a proprietary scraper, with which the carbon can be scraped and chipped from the head. See that the combustion chamber is not deeply scratched.

Remove all traces of carbon from the interior surfaces and do not forget the sparking plug hole and the valve ports. Carbon forms less readily on a smooth surface and therefore it is a good plan to polish the inside of the head with fine emery cloth, but do this before removing the valves, and afterwards remove all abrasive particles, using paraffin or petrol. Also

---

* When replacing old rings, it is generally inadvisable to clean the backs of the rings or the vertical faces of the grooves.

scrape all carbon from the valve heads. The ports and underside of the valve heads cannot be cleaned until the valves are removed (*see* below).

In the case of the O.H.V. head, care should be taken that the ground joint of the head is not damaged. The method adopted at the works of holding the head while decarbonizing is to fit a hexagon steel bar screwed at one end into the sparking plug hole. The cylinder head may then be held in a vice by means of the steel bar. If such a bar (*see* Fig. 51) is not available, an old sparking plug makes a useful substitute. This will facilitate the operation considerably.

With the comparatively soft aluminium-alloy piston be very careful when removing carbon deposits. On no account use emery cloth, but scrape off the deposits with a proprietary scraper or a blunt screwdriver. Avoid scratching the piston crown deeply, and afterwards wipe the surface with a rag moistened with paraffin or petrol (*see also* page 92).

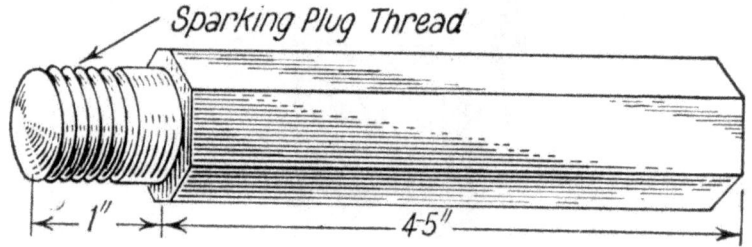

Fig. 51. A Hexagon Steel Bar Turned and Threaded at one End to Hold the Cylinder Head when Decarbonizing

Do not attempt to remove carbon from the skirt. Some carbon is usually deposited on the *inside of the piston*. If a piston is removed, this should be cleaned off. The screwdriver can be used for this till all carbon is scraped off ribs, etc., inside the piston. Take care not to let the screwdriver shank bump against the piston skirt, or the latter may crack. Examine the rings and grooves for carbon. But do not scrape it off the backs of *old* rings and from the bottom of the grooves in which they fit. For cleaning piston-ring grooves, use a proprietary groove scraper, a piece of broken ring (with one end ground to a Vee) attached to a handle, or a broken hacksaw blade. Wash the piston and rings thoroughly in clean paraffin or petrol. Refit the rings either by slipping them over the piston or with the three strips previously described.

Removing Valves (Side-by-side Type). Each valve may be removed while the cylinder is on the crankcase or after detaching the cylinder barrel, by means of a proprietary spring compressor such as the model illustrated in Fig. 52 (*A*). This should be placed, after removing the cylinder head, so that the hook rests on the valve head. The lever portion should be placed under the valve spring cap and the lever depressed; when the spring is lifted to its full extent, fix the ratchet arm in position. Both hands are now free to remove the valve cotters. If stiff, tap the outer collar. Split-type valve cotters are fitted, and these may be easily removed with the fingers. Remove the valve-lifter tool; the valve can then be withdrawn and the duplex spring and collars removed.

Removal of Valves (Overhead Type). This can be accomplished with the aid of a tool, such as the handy O.H.V. valve spring compressor shown in

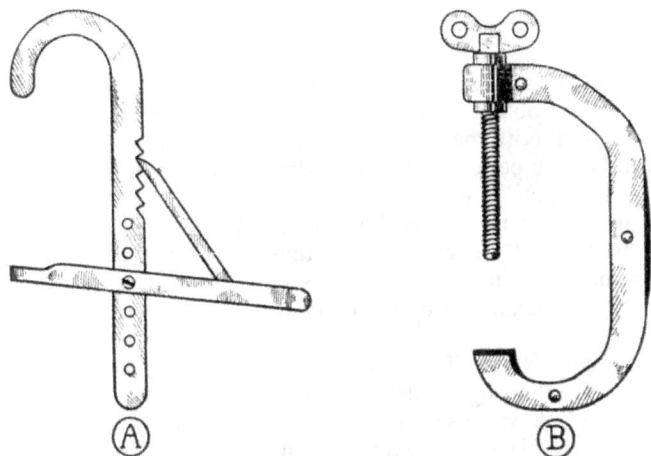

FIG. 52. TWO USEFUL VALVE SPRING COMPRESSORS

Both the above types are suitable for Norton engines. That shown at *A* is for S.V. engines and that at *B* for O.H.V engines.

Fig. 52 (*B*). To remove the split-type valve cotters on all O.H.V. engines (or on the S.V. engines) place the spring compressor with the forked end resting on the valve spring outer cap, and the end of the screw in the centre of the valve. Then tighten the screw (and tap forked end) until the spring is compressed enough to enable the split cotters to be removed. The valve can then be drawn out and the springs and collars removed.

Grinding-in the Valves. Should the valve faces or seats show signs of serious pitting, the valves will have to be ground-in.* Do not grind them in whenever you decarbonize, as excessive grinding causes the valves to become "pocketed." About once every 10,000 miles should be sufficient if

---

* Always grind-in valves when renewing them, and before grinding-in valves which have seen much service, always check that the valve stems and guides are not excessively worn.

the valve clearances are correctly maintained. Valves of the side-by-side type have, of course, to be *pressed down* on their seatings when using a screwdriver, while those of the overhead type have to be pulled up against their seatings with a hand vice, or pressed down with a suction tool.

Only grind-in a valve when necessary, using a proprietary *medium grade* valve grinding paste; only a small quantity is necessary, and do not revolve the valve round and round, but give a quarter turn backwards and forwards, frequently raising the valve from its seat and dropping it down in a different position.

The two valve stems may be cleaned but *they should not be polished.* Do not use coarse grinding compound for grinding-in. Some medium paste smeared very lightly over the valve face is far better. Richford's grinding paste is very suitable. Never continue grinding-in after a good seating has been obtained. All pitting should disappear and there should be a perfectly smooth matt ring round the face of the valve and the valve seating, indicating perfect contact. Depth of contact does not matter and about $\frac{1}{32}$ in. is quite sufficient.

After grinding-in the valves, be most careful to remove every trace of grinding paste. In the event of the pitting being very extensive and deep, it may be necessary to have the valves refaced and the seats recut by a Norton repair specialist or by the manufacturers.

Replacing the Valves. The inlet and exhaust valves must not be interchanged. Clean thoroughly the valve guides, the valve seats, and the valve ports. Also oil the valve stems which must be quite clean, but preferably not polished. Replace each valve and fit the duplex spring and collars. With the appropriate valve spring compressor (*see* page 81), compress the valve spring until the split collet can be inserted between the outer collar and the groove on the valve stem. Greasing the halves of the split collet will facilitate assembly.

Grinding-in a Cylinder Head. It occasionally happens that the metal-to-metal joint between an O.H.V. cylinder head and barrel "blows" because of superficial damage (scratches) on one or both joint surfaces. If the head is of *cast iron* the joint can safely be reconditioned by applying some grinding paste (coarse and then fine) to the barrel or head face and then grinding-in the faces by turning the head by hand backwards and forwards (not right round) until perfectly smooth joint faces are obtained. Every so often, wipe the paste off and smear some new grinding paste on the joint face. Deep scratches cannot, of course, be removed in this manner. After grinding-in is completed, be absolutely sure to remove *all* traces of the abrasive compound.

The Piston (1938–47). The correct piston ring gaps are on page 79. The side clearance, measured with a feeler, of the rings in their grooves should be 0·002 in. Check the rings in the cylinder bore for gap by placing each ring in the bore and pushing it down square by means of the piston.

The correct piston clearances (at the top of skirt) are for Model 16H, 0·0067 in. to 0·0057 in.; for Model 1, 0·0075 in. to 0·0065 in.; and for Models 18 and ES2, 0·0085 in. to 0·0075 in.

When replacing the piston, fit the piston to the connecting-rod in the same position as before and fit *new* circlips. Then proceed to fit the cylinder barrel.

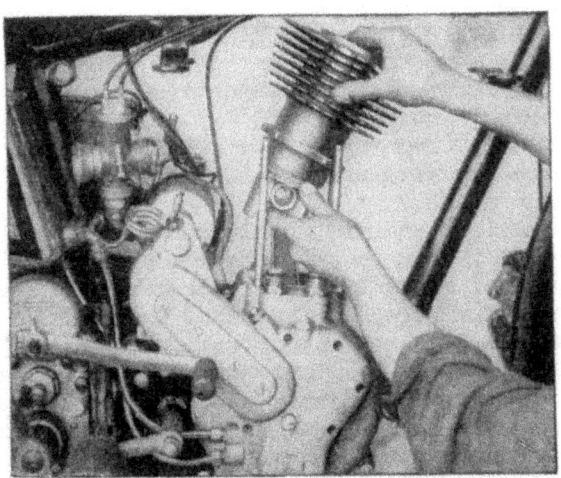

FIG. 53. REFITTING CYLINDER BARREL (O.H.V.)

If difficulty is experienced in getting the piston rings to enter the cylinder, get someone to hold the cylinder. See that the ring slots are spaced at 120 degrees and avoid damaging the elongated studs on 1938 and later O.H.V. models.

Replacing the S.V. Cylinder Barrel, etc. (1938–47). It is assumed that the piston rings are positioned on the piston with their gaps spaced equally apart. Oil the piston, rings, and cylinder bore. Then turn the engine until the connecting-rod big-end bearing is near its highest position, with the piston and connecting-rod pointing towards the front frame tube.

Replace the paper washer over the crankcase mouth and make certain that it does not obstruct the oil feed hole to the rear of the cylinder. Now fit the cylinder barrel over the piston, being careful to keep it square with the piston. Ease the barrel down over the piston while compressing the rings by hand. Assistance may be needed. Then tighten the cylinder-base securing nuts firmly and evenly.

Next fit the exhaust-valve lifter spindle to the cylinder barrel, complete with felt washer and spring. Place the milled end under the collar of the exhaust tappet, so that when the spindle is turned, the tappet is raised. To secure the spindle, replace the set-pin. Afterwards fit the exhaust-valve lifter cable adjuster to the cylinder, and also the return spring. Fit the exhaust-valve lifter cable to the actuating arm, and finally adjust the inlet and exhaust tappets to give the correct valve clearances (*see* page 70).

Replacing the O.H.V. Cylinder Barrel, Cylinder Head, Rocker-box, etc. (1938–47). Verify that the piston ring gaps are equally spaced, and oil the rings, piston, and the bore of the cylinder barrel. Next rotate the engine until the piston and big-end are near T.D.C., with the connecting-rod and piston pointing towards the front frame tube. Fit the paper washer over the mouth of the crankcase, being careful to see that the oil hole on the crankcase face is not masked.

Using assistance if necessary, ease the cylinder barrel over the piston, and slide it down the piston and barrel-fixing studs (*see* Fig. 53). Push the cylinder barrel right home.

Next, clean the cylinder barrel and cylinder-head joint faces. If no joint washer is specified, smear the contacting face with some oil. If a joint washer is provided, replace it. Then replace the cylinder head itself, fit the retaining nuts, and tighten the latter firmly and evenly.

Fit the two rocker-box distance pieces on the cylinder head (*see* Fig. 48) and fit paper washers on the distance pieces. No washers are required between the distance pieces and the cylinder head. Now fit the rocker-box itself and its retaining bolts and nuts. Tighten the nuts evenly and securely.

Having replaced the rocker-box, proceed to replace the two push-rods and push-rod cover tubes in precisely their former position. Be very careful to see that the rubber oil seal is properly fitted to the rocker-box. Then fit the rocker-box cover, taking special care to see that no rubber is trapped between the joint faces of the rocker-box and the cover. If the exhaust-valve lifter cable has been disconnected at the rocker-box, re-connect it. Finally adjust the push-rods to give the correct valve clearances (*see* page 71), and replace the petrol tank as described on page 74.

DECARBONIZING 1948–56 MODELS

For the reasons stated on page 73, it is advisable to decarbonize your Norton engine about every 5,000–8,000 miles (no precise mileage can be stated), but the *valves should not be ground-in more often than is necessary*. Inspect them, however, at each decarbonizing.

Petrol Tank Removal. You need not bother to remove the tank from your S.V. Model 16H or 1 Norton in order to decarbonize the piston, but if you wish to remove the cylinder barrel so as to have a look at the piston and rings, you *must* remove the tank. If you are about to "decoke" an O.H.V. Model 18, 19, 19R, ES2, or 50, you must take the tank off, whether

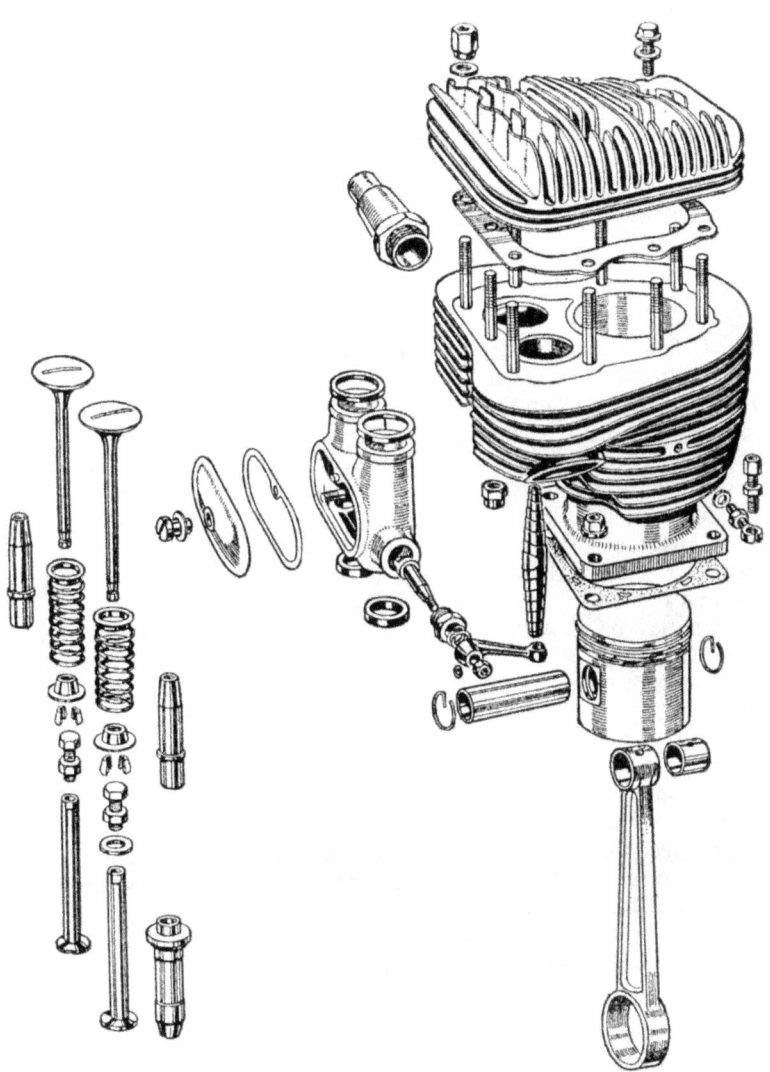

Fig. 54. Exploded View Showing Part of S.V. Engine (1948–54)

(*Norton Motors, Ltd.*)

An exploded view of the lower part of the engine is shown in Fig. 66.

you desire to withdraw the cylinder barrel or not. Detailed advice for removing and fitting the petrol tank is given on page 73.

To Remove S.V. Cylinder Head (1948 Onwards). First take off the petrol tank (*see* above) if you desire subsequently to remove the cylinder barrel. On a Model 16H or 1, remove the h.t. lead from the 14 mm sparking plug, and the plug itself. Then unscrew the nine nuts which secure the light-alloy cylinder head to the cylinder barrel. Now carefully lift off the cylinder head and also the head gasket. It is not desirable to remove the cylinder barrel every time you decarbonize.

Removing S.V. Cylinder Barrel (1948–54). Having removed the petrol tank (*see* page 73), you can remove the cylinder head and barrel from your Model 16H or 1 engine either separately or together. It is assumed here that the cylinder head has already been removed from the barrel (*see* Fig. 54). Next slacken the screw which secures the Amal carburettor to the induction stub by means of a clip. Pull the carburettor right off and allow it to hang suspended by the control cables. Detach the exhaust pipe or complete exhaust system.

Remove the valve-chest cover and rotate the engine until the piston is at B.D.C. with both valves closed. Now detach the exhaust-valve lifter control cable from the arm below the exhaust port by elevating the arm and then releasing the cable. This frees the return spring and the cable adjuster may be unscrewed from the cylinder barrel, so completely disconnecting the cable. Then unscrew the hexagon-headed bush housing the valve-lifter spindle and remove the exhaust-valve lifter itself from the valve chest.

Free the cylinder barrel by removing the four nuts from the crankcase studs and then lift the barrel off while supporting the valve chest with one hand. As may be seen in Fig. 54, the chest is an entirely separate casting. Be careful with the washers and renew them if not perfect. The washer fitted between the crankcase and cylinder barrel is of paper, but composition washers are used to make an oil-tight (top) joint between the valve chest and cylinder barrel. Rubber washers are provided for the bottom joints.

After removing the cylinder barrel, block up the crankcase mouth with a large clean cloth, so as to prevent dirt entering.

To Remove O.H.V. Rocker-box, Cylinder Head and Barrel (1948–54) The correct procedure for stripping down your Model 18 or ES2 engine for "decoking" it is as follows. Having taken off the petrol tank (*see* page 73), slacken the screw on the clip securing the Amal carburettor to the induction stub and withdraw the carburettor, allowing it to hang on the control cables. Next, with the "C" spanner in the tool-kit (Fig. 36), unscrew the exhaust pipe locking ring and remove the exhaust pipe or the entire exhaust system as a unit. Also disconnect at the rocker-box banjo the oil feed pipe shown at (4) in Fig. 23.

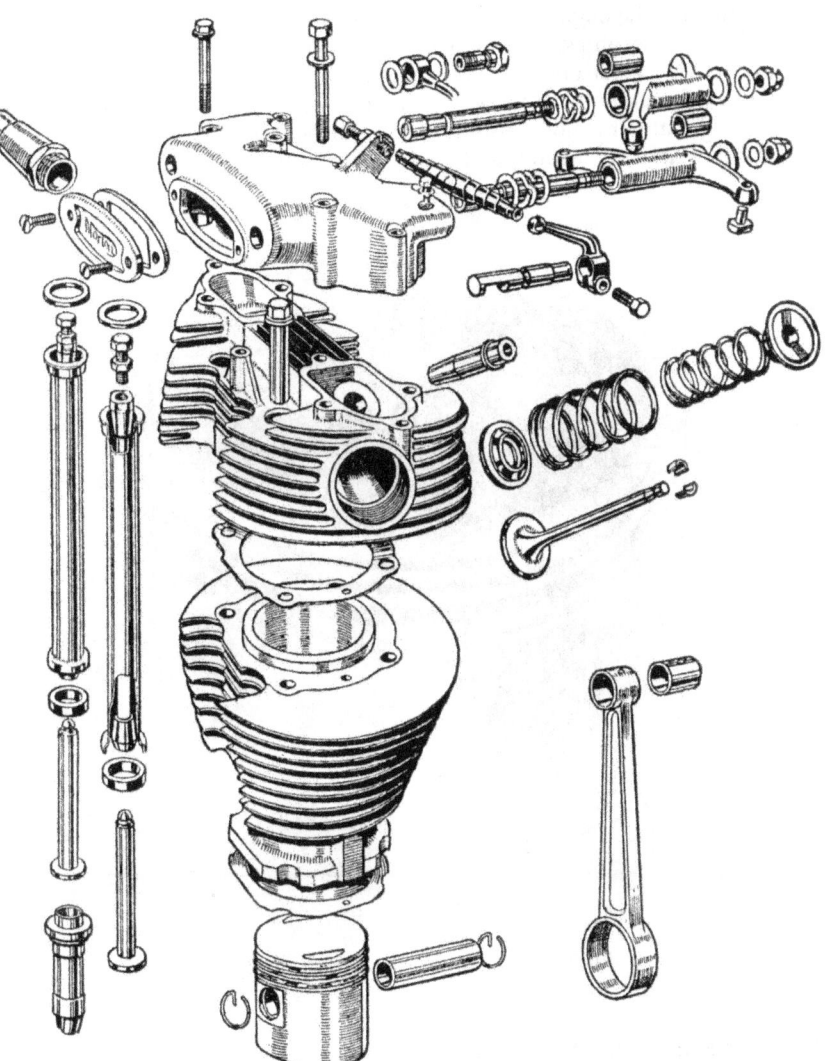

Fig. 55. Exploded View Showing Upper Part of O.H.V. Engine (1948 Onwards)

(*Norton Motors, Ltd.*)

An exploded view of the lower part of the crankcase is shown in Fig. 66. On 1955 and later engines the top face of the light-alloy cylinder head (*see* Fig. 59) has nine vertical studs, and nuts are used to secure the rocker-box. 1948–54 O.H.V. engines employ bolts as shown above.

Now turn the engine over until the piston is at T.D.C. with both valves closed, and disconnect the h.t. lead and remove the plug. Then proceed to remove the rocker-box from the cylinder head (*see* Fig. 55). To do this, loosen the nine bolts which secure the rocker-box and detach those which can be got at. It is not possible to remove the three centre rear bolts until the box is actually taken off. To take the rocker-box off, support with one

FIG. 56. PISTON REMOVED FROM O.H.V. ENGINE (PRE-1956)
The gudgeon-pin (Fig. 57) and the three rings (Fig. 58) have been removed.

hand the top ends of both the push-rod cover-tubes, raise the rocker-box approximately $\frac{1}{4}$ in., and then detach it from the cylinder head. The box can be removed completely or left hanging on the exhaust-valve lifter control cable.

After removing the rocker-box, remove both the push-rod cover-tubes and the push-rods. When withdrawing the cover-tubes, be careful not to lose the composition washers and rubber washers from the top and bottom ends respectively. Renew the washers if damaged. Do not mix up the inlet and exhaust push-rods and covers; they should later be replaced in their original positions.

To remove the cylinder head, unscrew the four securing nuts and withdraw the head from the spigot of the cylinder barrel. If the joint is stiff,

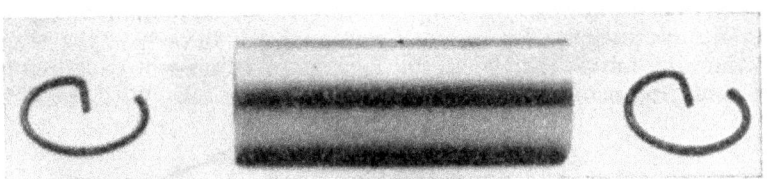

Fig. 57. Showing Gudgeon-pin Removed from Piston, and the Two Circlips

apply some sharp taps with a mallet or wooden implement (just below the inlet port).

As on the S.V. engines, it is not essential to withdraw the cylinder barrel each time the engine is decarbonized, as carbon can be scraped from the piston with the barrel in position. If you wish to inspect the piston and

Fig. 58. The 1956 Flat-top Wire-wound Piston
(*By courtesy of "The Motor Cycle," London*)
Note the slotted oil-control ring.

rings, turn the engine over until the piston is at B.D.C. and then lift the cylinder barrel off vertically. When doing this, support the piston with one hand as it emerges from the mouth of the barrel, and cover up the crankcase mouth with a clean cloth to prevent the possible entry of foreign matter.

To Remove O.H.V. Rocker-box, Cylinder Head and Barrel (1955 Onwards). The dismantling procedure for decarbonizing a Model ES2, 19R, 19S, or 50 is as follows. First remove the petrol tank as described on page 73. Then proceed to remove the rocker-box and cylinder head *together*.

Remove the two nuts securing the "monobloc" carburettor flange to the face on the light-alloy cylinder head, and withdraw the carburettor. The air and throttle slides need not be withdrawn unless it is desired to dismantle the carburettor for cleaning (*see* page 54). With the "C"

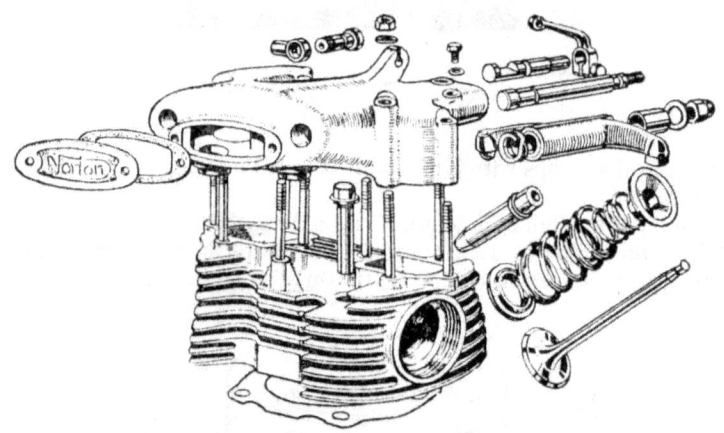

FIG. 59. CYLINDER HEAD AND ROCKER-BOX DETAILS ON O.H.V. ENGINES (1955 ONWARDS)
For cylinder barrel, push-rod, and cover-tube details, *see* Fig. 55.

spanner in the tool-kit (Fig. 36A) unscrew the exhaust-pipe finned locking-ring and remove the exhaust pipe or the complete exhaust system in one piece. Disconnect the oil-delivery pipe and the exhaust-valve lifter cable from the rocker-box.

Rotate the engine slowly until the piston is at T.D.C. with both valves closed, and disconnect the h.t. lead and remove the sparking plug. Now unscrew the four cylinder-head retaining nuts and, standing on the near side, lift the rocker-box and light-alloy head clear of the cylinder barrel spigot. When doing this, get someone to hold the two push-rods and cover-tubes. It is important not to mix up the push-rods, as they must be assembled in their original positions. Be careful not to lose the rubber and composition washers from the push-rod cover-tube ends.

Having removed the rocker-box and cylinder head together, separate them. Remove the nine nuts securing the rocker-box to the head and lift the rocker-box clear of the cylinder head studs.

If you wish to remove the cylinder barrel (not advised at every decarbonizing) in order to inspect the piston and rings, turn the engine over slowly until the piston is at B.D.C. and lift the barrel off vertically. As the piston emerges, support it with one hand and cover up the crankcase mouth to prevent dirt or foreign bodies entering the crankcase.

Removing the Piston. Unlike some earlier pistons, the type used for 1948 onwards is of the flat-top type. On Models 16H, 1, 18, ES2, 19R, 19S, it gives a compression ratio of 4·9, 4·5, 6·6, 6·8, 6·2, and 6·2 to 1 respectively.* Two compression rings and one oil control ring are fitted. Holes in the oil control ring groove allow surplus oil to be returned to the inside of the piston. As may be seen in Figs. 56 and 58, the piston crown on all O.H.V. engines has two grooves, fore and aft, to prevent any possibility of the valves fouling it. On both S.V. and O.H.V. engines the piston is of light alloy, and therefore great care must be taken to prevent its being scratched or damaged.

To remove the piston after withdrawing the cylinder barrel as already described, you must first remove the circlips, using a suitable pair of pliers such as the 6 in. pliers (*see* page 61) obtainable from a Norton spares stockist. It will be noticed in Fig. 57 that the gudgeon-pin circlips are of stout design and that only *one* end of a circlip can be gripped with the pliers.

The correct technique for removing a gudgeon-pin circlip is to grip the turned-in end of the circlip with the pliers and then pull simultaneously *outwards and towards the centre*. Using this method, the circlip should leave the annular groove in the piston boss readily. It is important when removing a circlip in the above manner to *hold the piston firmly* with one hand so as to prevent any side strain being imposed on the connecting-rod, also to block up the crankcase mouth. A circlip falling inside the crankcase may cause horrible trouble. As soon as you remove a circlip, scrap it. A new one *must always* be used on assembly.

Having removed the circlips, push out the fully floating gudgeon-pin. It is a running fit in both the reamed piston bosses and the small-end bearing of the connecting-rod. It is essential to replace the piston in its original position. Therefore mark it on the inside in a suitable manner (*see* Fig. 49) so as to ensure its correct replacement.

Valve Removal. It is not desirable to grind-in the valves every time the engine is decarbonized (*see* page 81), but if there is poor compression, loss of power, and hissing is detected on turning the engine over against compression, they should be removed and ground-in. Instructions for removing the valves from the cylinder barrel of a S.V. engine, or from the cylinder head of an O.H.V. engine, are given on pages 80–81, and on page

---

* On the 1956 Models 19S, ES2, 50 the compression ratios are 6·4, 7·1, and 7·3 to 1 respectively.

81 suitable types of valve spring compressors for S.V. and O.H.V. engines are illustrated.

If no valve spring compressor is available, remove the valves by inverting the cylinder barrel or head on the bench, with packing interposed between the valve heads and bench, and then pressing down on each outer valve spring collar (with a spanner) until the split collet can be detached from the valve stem. Be careful not to mix up the inlet and exhaust valves, which must *always* be replaced on their original ground-in seats.

Inspecting and Removing Piston Rings. Note the instructions given on page 78, especially those concerning the removal of the rings from the piston. Being made of light-alloy, the piston as well as the rings is likely to suffer by careless removal of the latter. Use the safe method shown in Fig. 50 to remove the two compression rings and the (bottom) oil control ring. The oil control ring (*see* Fig. 58) can be fitted either way up.

If the rings are in good condition, as revealed by a visual inspection, do not touch them. Also make no attempt to remove carbon from the backs of the rings or from the base of each ring groove.

Always check new piston rings for size in their grooves, by inserting a feeler gauge between each ring and an adjacent land. The correct side clearance is 0·002 in. If the cylinder bore wear exceeds 0·005–0·008 in., it is useless to fit new standard rings, and the cylinder requires to be rebored and an oversize piston and rings fitted. As regards the correct ring gaps (with rings pushed down squarely into the cylinder bore), those specified on page 82 do not apply to 1948–56 S.V. and O.H.V. engines. The gaps on being checked with a feeler gauge should measure 0·012–0·016 in. for both compression rings, and 0·005 in. for the oil-control (scraper) ring.

Removing Carbon Deposits. Follow the general instruction given on pages 79–80 and scrape off all carbon deposits from the piston and cylinder head. There are certain points which should be noted. On the 1948–54 S.V. engines and 1955–6 O.H.V. engines, the cylinder head is made of light alloy and therefore *no abrasive*, such as emery cloth, should be used to polish the combustion chamber surfaces. The O.H.V. cylinder head has an aluminium gasket; be careful not to damage this.

The advice given on page 82 regarding grinding-in the cylinder head and barrel does not apply, but the method of holding the cylinder head when decarbonizing, advocated on page 80, is recommended. Carbon deposits accumulated inside the valve ports and the valve spring compartments cannot be scraped off until the valves are removed, but removal is not advised too frequently (*see* page 81).

When undertaking a top overhaul (i.e. when *not* removing the cylinder barrel) it is a good plan before scraping carbon deposits off the piston to lay an old compression ring on top of the piston and inside the top of the bore. This will prevent removal of the carbon from the end of the bore and the top edge of the piston. Carbon here acts as an oil seal and is beneficial, especially after a considerable mileage. Removal of such carbon may temporarily increase the oil consumption.

Grinding-in the Valves. Do this not more often than is necessary, and do not grind-in the valves excessively on their 45 degree seats. Appropriate instructions are given on page 81. See that the valves are ground-in on their original seats after removing all carbon from both sides of the valve heads and from the valve stems protruding from the valve guides.

To Replace the Valves. Fit the valves (in their correct seats), the valve springs, collars, and split collets, as described on page 82.

Replacing Piston Rings and Piston. Fit the two compression rings and the oil-control ring to the piston, if these have been removed. It is advisable to oil the piston-ring grooves first and to fit the rings in the same manner as they were removed (*see* Fig. 50). The oil-control piston ring, shown in Fig. 58, must be fitted in the *bottom* groove and it can be replaced either way up.

Verify that the ring gaps are correct (*see* page 92) and then offer up the piston, with rings fitted, to the small-end of the connecting-rod. Make quite certain that the piston is fitted exactly in its original position. This is vitally important.

Oil the gudgeon-pin (Fig. 57) and insert this (in its original position) into the piston bosses and small-end bush of the connecting-rod. Push the gudgeon-pin right home against the circlip and then with a pair of pliers (*see* page 61) fit the second *new* circlip. See that it beds down properly in its groove. Now all is ready for the cylinder barrel to be fitted.

Replacing S.V. Cylinder Barrel (1948–54). Before fitting the cylinder barrel arrange the piston rings so that the three gaps are equally spaced (i.e. at 120 degrees to each other). Also smear some clean engine oil on the inside of the cylinder bore, and on the piston and rings. Turn the engine slowly until the piston is close to T.D.C. with the connecting-rod inclined towards the front down-tube of the frame.

Unless in perfect condition, renew the paper washer on the mouth of the crankcase. When fitting the washer be careful not to obstruct the orifice of the oil feed hole which registers with the hole in the cylinder barrel, responsible for lubricating the rear of the cylinder. Referring to Fig. 54, replace the two rubber washers on the tappet guides. Also fit the two composition washers to the upper side of the detachable valve chest. Then locate the valve chest, with washers in position, on the top face of the crankcase.

Hold the cylinder barrel over the piston and offer up the piston. Obtain some assistance to ease the piston rings into the mouth of the cylinder and to support the valve chest, both of which are necessary. It is desirable to use some jointing compound for the cylinder-base joint.

After checking that the valve chest *is* truly located, proceed to tighten down the four nuts which secure the cylinder barrel to the crankcase. Do not forget to fit the spring washers, and tighten the nuts in a diagonal order and evenly. Now replace the exhaust-valve lifter mechanism. See that the actuating part is properly located below the exhaust tappet washer. Replace the control-cable adjuster and the valve-lifter return spring. Then reconnect the cable to the exhaust-valve lifter lever. Finally check and if necessary adjust the valve clearances as described on page 70, and refit the valve-chest cover.

Fitting S.V. Cylinder Head (1948-54). The light-alloy cylinder head on a Model 16H or 1 side-valve engine can be replaced in a few minutes. Before replacing the head, inspect the joint washer closely for evidence of "blowing" or damage. Renew this washer at once if not in perfect condition.

Pass the cylinder head over the nine securing studs on the barrel and then fit the spring washers and securing nuts. Tighten all nine nuts finger-tight first and then evenly in a diagonal order with a spanner until they are firmly retightened. Afterwards replace the sparking plug and the h.t. lead.

To Replace O.H.V. Cylinder Barrel, Cylinder Head, and Rocker-box (1948-54). First arrange the piston rings so that the gaps of the rings are equally spaced (120 degrees). Next smear some clean engine oil on the piston, rings, and cylinder bore. Turn the engine over until the piston is near T.D.C. Fit the paper washer to the mouth of the crankcase and see that it is undamaged and does not obstruct the oil hole for lubricating the rear of the cylinder. Apply jointing compound to both washer faces.

Place the cylinder barrel over the four long crankcase studs and as it reaches the piston, ease the rings carefully into the cylinder mouth. Gently slide the barrel right home.

Examine the joint faces for the cylinder head and see that they are scrupulously clean. Replace the aluminium gasket on the joint face of the cylinder barrel. Then fit the cylinder head and firmly and evenly (diagonally) tighten the four cylinder-head securing nuts.

To replace the rocker-box, position the three rear-centre bolts in the rocker-box and locate the rocker-box on the top face of the cylinder head. Before doing this, however, do not forget to smear some jointing compound on the two mating faces. Next replace loosely the remaining rocker-box securing bolts and correctly locate the push-rods and push-rod cover-tubes. See that the washers for the cover-tubes are replaced in their original positions. The rubber washers must be at the bottom and the composition washers at the upper ends. Tighten all the rocker-box securing bolts firmly and evenly (diagonally), and then replace the sparking plug and the oil-feed pipe to the rocker-box. Finally remove the oval-shaped rocker-box inspection cover, adjust the valve clearances (nil) as described on page 71, and replace the cover.

To Replace O.H.V. Cylinder Barrel, Rocker-box, and Cylinder Head (1955 Onwards). First replace the cylinder barrel exactly as described on page 94 for the 1948 to 1954 O.H.V. engines.

After sliding the barrel home over the long crankcase studs, carefully clean the top face of the cylinder head and the bottom face of the rocker-box. Smear some jointing compound on both faces, but avoid using an excessive amount. Position the four sleeve-nuts which retain the cylinder barrel and head, and carefully fit the rocker-box (Fig. 59) over the cylinder head studs, and press the box home. Fit all nine nuts and washers securing the rocker-box, but preferably defer final tightening down of these nuts until the cylinder head and rocker-box have been assembled to the cylinder barrel.

Clean the bottom face of the light-alloy cylinder head and the top face of the cylinder barrel. Also fit the aluminium gasket (*see* Fig. 55) to the cylinder barrel face. Then offer up the assembled cylinder head and rocker-box to the cylinder barrel. When doing this get an assistant to hold the inlet and exhaust push-rods and cover-tubes in position, and to engage the upper and lower ends of the push-rods with the ball ends of the overhead rockers and the tappet cups respectively. Make sure that the inlet and exhaust push-rods are not interchanged; see that the rubber washers are fitted to the lower ends of the push-rod cover-tubes, and the composition washers to the upper ends of the cover-tubes. Now thread the cylinder barrel and head retaining nuts on the four crankcase studs and tighten these nuts down firmly and evenly (using a diagonal order).

Reconnect the oil-delivery pipe and the exhaust-valve lifter cable to the rocker-box. Adjust the cable adjuster as described on page 72 to give the requisite clearance between the rocker arm and the cam. Check the valve clearances (*see* page 71) and, if necessary, adjust the upper ends of the rods until the clearance is nil but the rods can freely rotate. Fit the rocker-box end cover.

Final Reassembly (S.V. and O.H.V.). Replace the exhaust pipe, or complete exhaust system if this has been removed. With the "C" spanner in the tool-kit screw the ring nut firmly into the threaded end of the exhaust port. Replace the Amal carburettor on the induction stub (1938–54), and see that it is quite vertical. Tighten the screw on the clip, or the two nuts securing the "monobloc" carburettor flange (1955 onwards), securely so as to prevent any air leaks.

Replace the petrol tank. Instructions for doing this are given on page 73. Note especially the correct assembly order for the mounting washers (shown in Fig. 46). Finally to complete the assembly, reconnect the petrol pipes to the float chamber of the carburettor. After a short mileage, check over the various nuts and bolts for tightness, and apply the appropriate spanners where necessary.

IGNITION AND VALVE TIMING

Ignition Timing. Exact ignition timing is extremely important. For all normal road uses, the spark settings given subsequently (*see* page 98) should be closely adhered to.

It should always be remembered that should the timing be so far advanced that maximum explosion pressures are reached with the crank in true T.D.C. position, the big-end comes in for a terrific hammering for which it is not designed.

Retiming the Lucas "Magdyno." If a "Magdyno" has been removed for any purpose or the drive disturbed, it will be necessary to retime it, and to do this proceed as follows.

It is assumed that the Lucas "Magdyno" has been replaced on its mounting (*see* page 102), but that the driving chain and the "Magdyno" and inlet-camshaft sprockets have not yet been fitted. Replace the two sprockets and the driving chain. Tap the inlet-camshaft sprocket home (*see* Fig. 63) on the taper and key. After tapping the sprocket home, tighten its securing nut firmly. Fit the nut securing the "Magdyno" sprocket, but keep the sprocket free on the taper and do not tighten the nut. Next engage top gear and move the ignition lever on the handlebars so that it is in the *fully advanced* position. Then slowly turn the engine with the rear wheel until the piston is exactly at top-dead-centre (T.D.C.) on the compression stroke, with both valves closed, as described below.

Remove the sparking plug (O.H.V. engines) or dummy plug (S.V. engines), and insert a thin rod or thick piece of wire through the plug hole. By slightly turning the engine backwards and forwards you can find the true T.D.C. position where no piston movement occurs. Scratch a mark on the rod or wire (if a wire is used, see that it does not bend) to indicate the T.D.C. position and then scratch another mark $\frac{7}{16}$ in. (or whatever the exact ignition advance is) *above* the first mark.

Rotate the engine very slowly *backwards* until the top mark occupies and just passes the position previously occupied by the bottom mark. Now turn the engine slowly *forward* until the top mark exactly occupies this position. The piston obviously has now descended a distance equivalent to the ignition advance ($\frac{7}{16}$ in. or whatever it is), with chain backlash removed (by turning the engine forward).

If the cylinder head is removed for decarbonizing, the ignition setting can be accurately set by laying a small plate or a straight-edge across the top face of the cylinder barrel and taking vertical measurements between the plate or straight-edge, and the piston crown, using a steel rule.

GENERAL MAINTENANCE

Without moving the piston, now set the contact-breaker so that its contacts are just beginning to open with the ignition lever fully advanced. To find the exact point when the contacts commence to open, place a *very* thin feeler gauge or a *very* thin piece of paper between the contacts so that the gauge or paper is gripped, and then cautiously turn the "Magdyno" armature *clockwise* (contact-breaker side) until the gauge or paper is just freed on exerting a gentle pull.

With the contacts at the point of "break," secure the "Magdyno" sprocket on the tapered shaft. To do this, hold a piece of tube over the

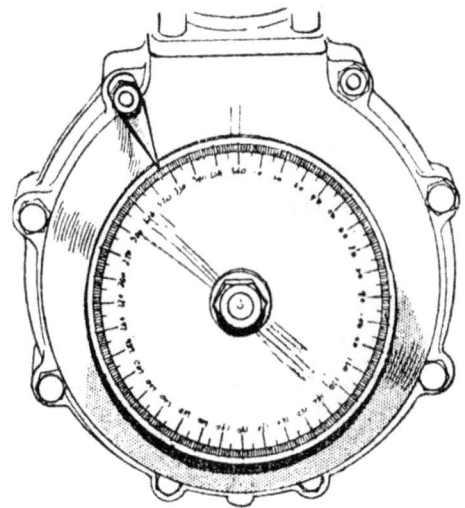

FIG. 60. CRANKSHAFT DEGREE-DISC FOR IGNITION AND VALVE TIMING

A suitable pointer can be fixed as shown to one of the crankcase bolts. The T.D.C. position must first be found.

shaft and against the sprocket, and then carefully tap the tube. This will force the sprocket *squarely* home on to the taper.* Now tighten the "Magdyno" sprocket securing-nut with the appropriate box spanner. When tightening the nut, do not hold the contact-breaker, or it may be damaged.

After checking, and if necessary adjusting, the ignition timing, set the gap between the contacts (*see* page 66), replace the contact-breaker cover, retension the "Magdyno" driving-chain if necessary (*see* page 103), and replace the "Magdyno" chain-case cover.

* To loosen a "Magdyno" driving sprocket, tap on its securing nut lightly. If this is not effective, use a proper extractor.

Degree Method of Ignition Timing. More precise ignition timing can be obtained by measuring the ignition advance in degrees of crankshaft rotation, but it is doubtful whether extreme accuracy is necessary except for racing purposes. A suitable degree disc can be made up or obtained from C. C. Wakefield & Co., Ltd., the makers of Castrol lubricants. Fig. 60 shows a degree disc in position.

Ignition Advance (1938–9 Models). On Model 16H the contacts should commence to break with the piston $\frac{5}{32}$ in. (25 degrees) before T.D.C. on full advance. On the "Big Four" the correct timing is $\frac{1}{4}$ in. (25 degrees) before T.D.C. on full advance. The timing on Models 18, 20, ES2 is $\frac{3}{4}$ in. (42 degrees) before T.D.C. on full advance for touring and $\frac{23}{32}$ in. (47 degrees) for racing. On Model 19 the timing is $\frac{23}{32}$ in. (42 degrees) before T.D.C. for touring and $\frac{7}{8}$ in. (47 degrees) for racing. With regard to the Models 50, 55 the correct spark advance is $\frac{11}{16}$ in.–$\frac{3}{4}$ in. (48–50 degrees) before T.D.C. on full advance.

1946–7 Ignition Timings. The correct ignition timings for Models 16H and the "Big Four" are $\frac{7}{16}$ in. and $\frac{3}{8}$ in. before T.D.C. respectively, with the ignition lever fully *advanced*. For Models 18 and ES2, the correct timing is $\frac{5}{8}$ in. before T.D.C., also with the ignition lever fully *advanced*.

Ignition Advance (1948–56 Models). On the S.V. Models 16H, 1, the "Magdyno" contacts should begin to open with the piston $\frac{7}{16}$ in. before T.D.C. with the ignition lever *fully advanced*. On the O.H.V. Models 18, ES2 the correct ignition timing is $\frac{5}{8}$ in. before T.D.C. on full advance. On Models 19R, 19S, and 50 the correct ignition timing is $\frac{11}{16}$ in. before T.D.C. on full advance.

Valve Timing. The original timing should *not* be interfered with. On all Norton engines the timing gears are appropriately marked on assembly to ensure correct reassembly of the camwheels. If the camwheels are always replaced in the correct positions relatively to the engine half-time pinion (also marked), the valve timing *must* be permanently correct. Sometimes (e.g. after fitting new camwheels or cams) it is desirable to check the valve timing. Note that on all 1938–47 engines inclusive the inlet camwheel is driven off the exhaust camwheel. On 1948 and later engines, however, the inlet and exhaust camwheels are both driven direct off the half-time engine pinion.

To Check the Valve Timing. As a rough check on the timing "rock" the engine gently backwards and forwards about the T.D.C. position on the *exhaust* stroke. The inlet valve should be observed to open, and the exhaust valve to close in quick succession. To check the timing accurately, first check that the valve clearances (*see* page 69) are correct. Also position the piston at T.D.C. on the *exhaust* stroke (not the compression stroke). Then by taking measurements on the piston stroke (*see* page 96) or by using the degree method (*see* Fig. 60), record the exact moment when the inlet valve begins to open before T.D.C., and the exhaust valve closes after T.D.C.

Note that unless really necessary, it is inadvisable to remove the engine pinion. Some pre-1948 engines have detachable cams, and it is essential to see that such cams are firmly screwed to the camwheels prior to re-assembly. In this section the removal and replacement of the timing-case cover are dealt with, but detailed instructions for the dismantling and assembling of the timing gears, etc. will be found on pages 106–108.

Where Timing Gears are Unmarked. If for some reason the timing gears are renewed and the new gears are unmarked, check that the correct valve timing is obtained. Place the piston at T.D.C. and mesh the exhaust cam-wheel with the engine pinion such that the exhaust valve is about to close. Similarly, mesh the inlet camwheel such that the inlet valve is about to open. Proceed to move each camwheel *one tooth* in the required direction until the correct valve timing is obtained. If difficulty is experienced in obtaining the exact timing, remove the engine pinion and replace it, using the next key-way until timing is in accordance with the specified figure. The effect of moving the engine pinion one key-way is equivalent to altering the timing by one-third of a tooth.

Valve Timing (1938–9 16H, 1, 18, 19, 20, ES2). The valve timing diagram shown in Fig. 61, is applicable to the whole 1938–9 S.V. and O.H.V. Norton range, except Models 50, 55, when timing is measured on the degree system, which is strongly advocated.

When timing valves by means of measurements taken on the piston stroke, there are certain variations which should be carefully noted. These variations are made clear in the caption below the illustration (*see* Fig. 61). Three keyways are provided on all engine pinions and, if the timing is disturbed, the keyway into which the key fits should be marked as well as the pinions. In the case of Models 50, 55 the inlet valve should open $\frac{5}{16}$ in.–$\frac{3}{8}$ in. (30–35 degrees) before T.D.C., and the exhaust valve should close $\frac{3}{8}$ in.–$\frac{7}{16}$ in. (35–40 degrees) after T.D.C.

1946–7 Valve Timings. On all 1946–7 side-valve and overhead-valve models the inlet valve opens the same distance before T.D.C. as the exhaust valve closes after T.D.C. For Model 16H it is $\frac{9}{32}$ in.; for the "Big Four," $\frac{3}{8}$ in.; for Models 18 and ES2, $\frac{5}{16}$ in. The general advice given on page 98 applies and retiming is simple, as the timing gears are normally marked for correct meshing. Exact timing is essential, and the valve clearances must be correct when checking it. When retiming engines which have the engine number followed by the suffix "Q," a 0·017 in. feeler gauge should be inserted between each cam and crankcase-rocker pad. Adjust the valve clearance afterwards with the feeler gauge in position.

Detailed instructions for assembling the timing gears and oil pump are given on pages 107–108. These apply to all 1946–7 S.V. and O.H.V. models.

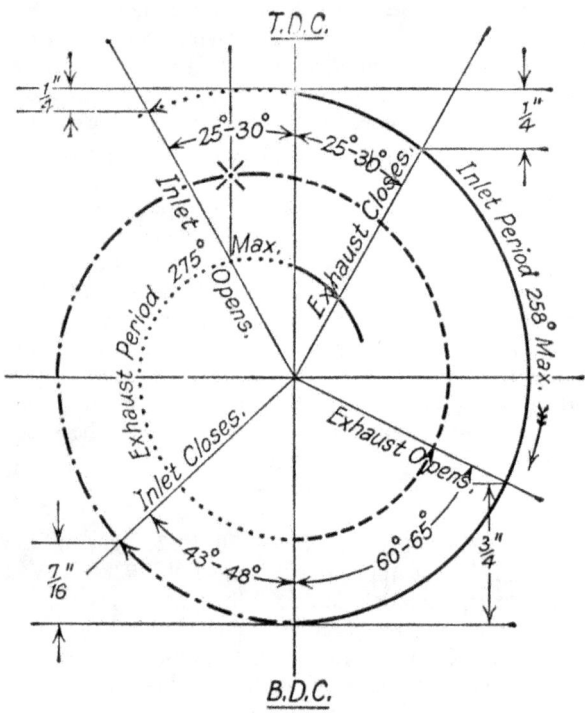

FIG. 61. VALVE-TIMING DIAGRAM FOR 1938–9 S.V. AND O.H.V. ENGINES

The valve-timing diagram shown is applicable to all 1938–9 S.V and O.H.V. engines except Models 50, 55, if timing be measured by degrees of crank rotation. The valve clearances must be correct when retiming. When timing is effected by measuring the distance between the piston crown and the dead centres, it should be noted that on the 5·96 h.p. and 6·33 h.p. long-stroke engines lessened connecting-rod angularity necessitates the exhaust valve opening being $\tfrac{1}{16}$ in. earlier and the other periods being increased to the extent of $\tfrac{1}{16}$ in.

1948–56 Valve Timings. For the 1948 and later engines, timings are: on Model 16H the inlet valve commences to open $\tfrac{9}{32}$ in. before T.D.C., and the exhaust valve closes $\tfrac{9}{32}$ in. after T.D.C. In the case of Model 1 the inlet valve begins to open $\tfrac{11}{32}$ in. before T.D.C., and the exhaust valve closes $\tfrac{11}{32}$ in. after T.D.C. On the O.H.V. Models 18 and ES2 the inlet valve begins to open $\tfrac{5}{16}$ in. before T.D.C., and the exhaust valve closes $\tfrac{5}{16}$ in. after T.D.C. On the O.H.V. Models 19R, 19S, and 50 the inlet valve begins to open $\tfrac{11}{32}$ in. before T.D.C., and the exhaust valve closes $\tfrac{11}{32}$ in. after T.D.C.

Removing Timing Cover (S.V., O.H.V. Engines). First unscrew the three cheese-headed screws and remove the "Magdyno" chain-case cover. Remove both sprockets with the chain in position. They are a taper fit,

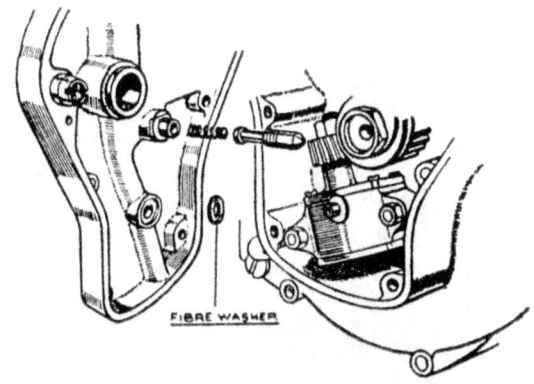

Fig. 62. Removal of Timing Cover and Restriction Jet

and the camwheel sprocket is also keyed. If difficulty in removal is experienced, use a suitable withdrawal tool. Then remove the timing cover, which is secured by six cheese-headed screws* and two counter-sunk screws, the latter being in the "Magdyno" chain case. Having removed all screws, partly withdraw the timing cover so as to expose the timing gears and rockers. To prevent the inlet camwheel and the rocker coming adrift, hold them in place with a screwdriver while completely withdrawing the timing cover. When the timing cover is removed, the restriction jet for the big-end will leave its holder because of the spring pressure behind it. Finally, remove the spring (see Fig. 62) from its holder. Be careful not to lose any shims fitted to the camwheel spindles.

Replacing Timing Cover (S.V., O.H.V.). To replace the timing cover on the S.V. and O.H.V. engines, first clean the edges of the timing cover and timing chest. Next smear the mating surfaces with some jointing compound or gold-size, and check the fibre washer (see Fig. 62) between the oil pump and the timing cover. Offer up the timing cover and verify that when in position the fibre washer prevents the edge of the cover contacting the

---

* It is important to note that the three top screws securing the timing cover are *shorter* than the three bottom ones.

timing chest by $\frac{1}{32}$ in. This spacing is necessary to ensure an oil-tight joint when the timing cover is screwed home and the washer is compressed. Finally, fit the spring and the restriction jet in its holder, and evenly and firmly tighten all the timing-cover securing screws.

ENGINE OVERHAUL

After an engine has been in service for a *very* long period and it becomes somewhat "rough," a complete overhaul is desirable. Some useful general instructions on engine overhaul are included in this section.

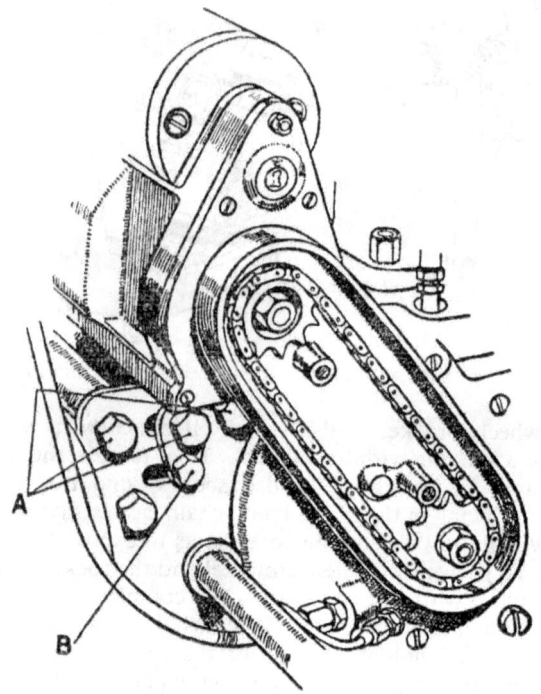

FIG. 63. SHOWING "MAGDYNO" SECURING BOLTS AND CHAIN DRIVE

The Lucas "Magdyno." It is advisable to return the complete instrument to a Lucas service depot for thorough inspection and overhaul, including regreasing of the bearings.

Removing and Replacing "Magdyno." It is advisable, first, to remove the engine-timing cover. Then remove the h.t. lead from the sparking plug and also the dynamo leads. Referring to Fig. 63, remove the locking

GENERAL MAINTENANCE

bolt *B* and the centre one of the three bolts *A*. Slacken the two outer bolts *A*. Now remove the Lucas "Magdyno." Replacement should be effected in the reverse order. Tightening of the bolts should be done *after* the timing cover has been replaced and the chain has been re-tensioned. Re-tensioning can be effected by moving the "Magdyno" in the required direction with the "Magdyno" security bolts slackened off. The total chain whip at the centre of the chain run should not exceed about $\frac{1}{4}$ in.

To Remove and Replace Dynamo. Removal of the dynamo from the "Magdyno" unit is dealt with on page 14.

The Sparking Plug. *See* pages 9 and 63–66.

Overhauling the Carburettor. Dismantling and inspection are dealt with on pages 52–57. For tuning instructions *see* page 47.

Assembling and Dismantling Twist-grip. Grease that portion of the handlebars on which the grip operates. Referring to Fig. 64, fit the sleeve to the bar. Apply some grease to the drum on the sleeve. Then fit the spring and adjuster bolt and nut to the lower half-clip. Pass the control cable through the clip hole and fit the nipple to the drum on the sleeve. Assemble the upper half-clip and adjust the twist-grip for tightness by means of the adjusting screw, afterwards locking it in the desired position. To dismantle the twist-grip, proceed in the reverse order of assembling.

The Ignition and Air Control Levers. Both are of identical design (*see* Fig. 64). To detach the control cable from the ignition or air lever, open the lever fully, hold the cable casing, and then, while closing the lever, pull the cable casing from the lever body. You can now detach the cable nipple from the lever. After removing the external dome-shaped bolt, the various parts can be dismantled as shown (exploded view) in Fig. 64.

When assembling the ignition or air lever, first grease both sides of the lever. To attach the cable, fit the nipple into the lever, close the lever, pull the cable casing away from the lever, and fit the cable to the lever body. Tighten the adjuster nut to give the correct degree of stiffness, and take up any slackness in the control cables.

The Exhaust-valve Lifter. To remove the control cable from the handlebar lever, turn the operating arm on the rocker-box by means other than pulling the cable, and detach the cable from the arm. Then detach the nipple from the handlebar lever and pass it through the large hole in the lever body. Be sure to fit the cable first to the handlebar lever when reassembling.

Removal of the Timing Gears and Oil Pump (1938–47). First on S.V. and O.H.V. models remove the timing cover as described in a previous paragraph. Then remove the two valve rockers, which, though identical,

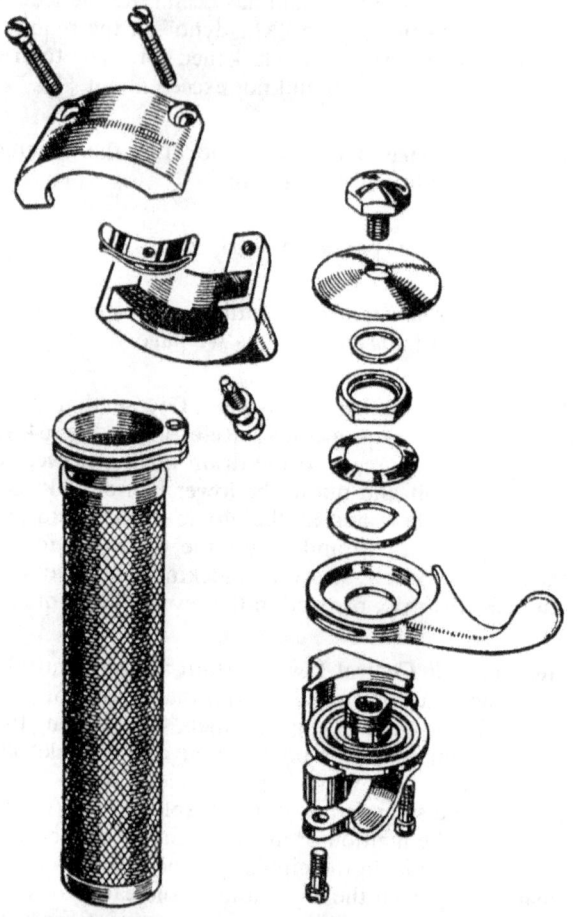

FIG. 64. COMPONENTS OF TWIST-GRIP AND AIR LEVER
The ignition lever assembly is the same as for the air lever.

should not be interchanged. Examine both valve rockers for wear at the contact areas, i.e. where they ride on the cams.

Withdraw the inlet camwheel, and proceed to remove the engine pinion nut which drives the oil pump (via a worm) and has a L.H. thread. Now withdraw the exhaust camwheel and remove the oil pump from the two studs after unscrewing the two securing nuts. The engine pinion can now (not before) be extracted if necessary.

Replacing the Timing Gears and Oil Pump (1938-47). If new timing gears are to be fitted to a S.V. or O.H.V. engine, check both camwheels for side-float. Detach the plug covering the end of the exhaust camwheel spindle. It is pressed into the timing cover. Next replace both camwheels, and fit and secure the timing cover, tightening all securing screws. Then check, in turn, the side-float of the inlet and exhaust camwheel spindles. The side-float of the inlet camwheel spindle can be felt on pushing and pulling the protruding spindle sideways. With the exhaust camwheel,

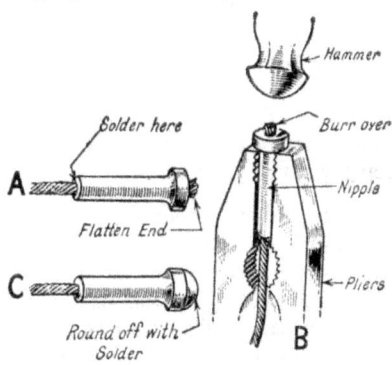

FIG. 65. How a Nipple Should be Soldered

Solder a nipple on to a control cable as shown in the order A, B, C.

insert tightly a tapered piece of steel (such as the tag end of a file) into the hollow camwheel spindle, and check for side-float in a similar manner. The correct side-float for both camwheels is 0·004 in. Excessive side-float can be rectified by fitting pen-steel washers to the camwheel spindles on each side of the camwheels. Having obtained correct side-float, remove the timing cover and press in the plug covering the end of the exhaust camwheel spindle.

Replace both rockers, and check with a feeler gauge the clearance between the face of each camwheel and the back of the corresponding rocker. The correct clearance is 0·006 in. Next remove the rockers and camwheels. If the engine pinion has been removed, replace it. Put the piston at T.D.C. In this position the key for the engine pinion should be at the bottom of the main-shaft, and of the three pinion key-ways, that should be used which causes the timing mark to be in the 2 o'clock position. Fit the exhaust camwheel and then the inlet camwheel, taking care to see that the timing marks register correctly. Afterwards fit both rockers and check the valve timing (*see* page 98). Fit the engine pinion (and pump-driving worm) nut. Then examine and fit the oil pump, replace the timing cover, fit the "Magdyno" driving chain and sprockets, tension the chain, and finally check the ignition timing.

Inspecting and Fitting Oil Pump. Unless absolutely essential, it is not recommended that the oil pump be stripped. It is advisable, however, when the pump has been removed to test for play in the spindle by pushing and pulling the worm wheel. By rotating the spindle while covering the oil holes with the fingers, it should be possible to feel the suction effect of the pump if it is in reasonably good condition. While actuating the pump, it should also be possible to feel any obstruction caused by the presence of foreign matter. Clean the pump thoroughly with paraffin before replacing it in the timing case.

It is assumed that the driving worm and nut (L.H. thread) has been fitted next to the engine pinion. Before fitting the pump itself, thoroughly clean the face to which the pump is to be fitted, and also the back of the pump. If jointing compound is used, employ only a light film and be most careful not to block up the oil holes. Examine and fit the fibre washer (*see* Fig. 62) between the pump feed and the timing cover.

To Dismantle Oil Pump When Essential. To take apart the oil pump fitted to the S.V. and O.H.V. models, remove the four cheese-head screws from the upper cover when the covers may be taken off, exposing the gears (Fig. 21). Before removing these, scratch or mark each gear to ensure correct replacement. The fitting of new parts is best undertaken by the manufacturers. End-play in the gears (i.e. between the end-face of the gears and the cover plate) must not exceed 0·002 in., and must not be too small or force will be required to rotate the driving-worm, and this will lead to wear on the worm and worm wheel.

Removing Timing Gears, Oil Pump, and Tappets (1948 Onwards). When the timing cover is removed as already described, the timing gears and the oil pump are exposed. Remove the nuts from the studs which retain the pump, and withdraw the pump unit (*see* Fig. 21). Next remove the oil pump driving-worm. This has a *left-hand thread*.

Withdraw the two camwheels (*see* Fig. 66) and see that any shims fitted to the ends of the spindles are put aside for correct reassembly. To remove the small engine pinion, use a sprocket withdrawal tool.

Do not remove the tappets unless this is essential, as their removal involves the removal of the pressed-in tappet guides. These have to be extracted with a sprocket drawer. If the tappets are taken out, see that they are not interchanged.

The Oil Pressure Control Valve. As stated on page 34, the valve should not normally be interfered with. Should any adjustment be made, the adjuster screw should afterwards be locked. The usual method of doing this is to punch a little of the aluminium into the screwdriver slot in the grub-screw.

GENERAL MAINTENANCE

Replacing Tappets, Timing Gears, and Oil Pump (1948 Onwards). If new camwheels are fitted, it is necessary to check their end float and reshim if necessary. When fully home in the timing case the sides of the camwheels must clear the boss housing the pressure-release valve. Add such shims as are necessary.

Replace the timing cover and push and pull on the inlet camwheel spindle and then shim-up until it is just possible to feel the endfloat. In the case of the exhaust camwheel, the end float of the spindle can only be properly estimated when the crankcase halves are parted.

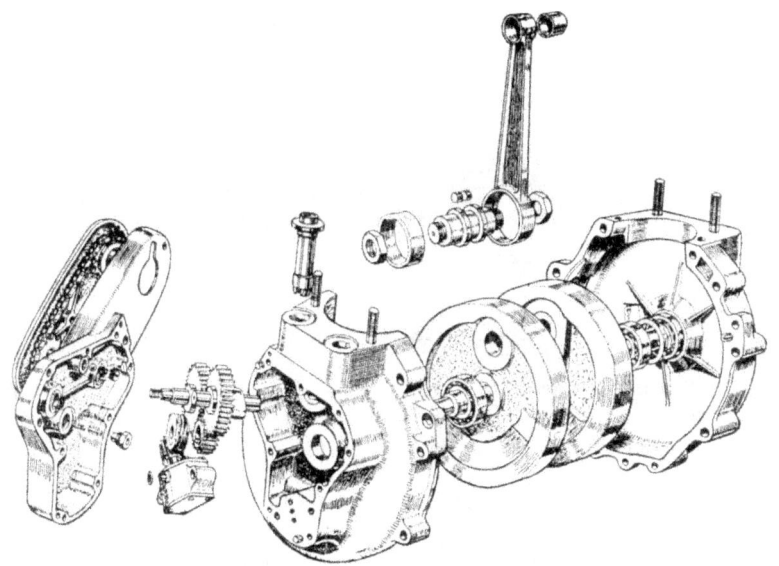

FIG. 66. EXPLODED VIEW SHOWING LOWER PART OF S.V. ENGINE (1948 ONWARDS)

(*Norton Motors, Ltd.*)

The arrangement on the O.H.V. engine is identical, except that long crankcase studs (*see* Fig. 53) are used to retain the cylinder barrel and cylinder head to the crankcase. Figs. 54 and 55 show exploded views of the upper part of the S.V. and O.H.V. engines respectively.

It is important to note that the inlet and exhaust tappets must be inserted into their guides *before* the guides are pressed home by means of a tubular drift. A peg in the top face of the crankcase enters a hole in the tappet guide collar, thereby locating each guide radially. Before tapping or pressing a guide home, see that the peg and hole are in alignment.

To assemble the timing gears, first fit the small engine pinion to the timing side main-shaft, and then turn the engine until the crankpin or piston is at T.D.C. Now replace the two camwheels (already shimmed-up).

See that the markings on the camwheel teeth correspond with those on the teeth of the small engine pinion. Incorrect meshing will result in the valve timing being wrong.

Replace and tighten the oil pump worm with a peg spanner or suitable punch. The worm has a *left-hand thread*. Then replace the oil pump itself. See that the two faces are quite clean. Avoid using excessive jointing compound which might obstruct the oil holes. Examine and fit the fibre washer (Fig. 62) on the oil pump nipple, and finally replace the timing cover (*see* page 101). Also retime the Lucas "Magdyno" (*see* page 96).

Removal of Timing Gear Bushes. A close inspection of the timing-gear bushes may reveal wear which calls for the renewal of the bushes. The

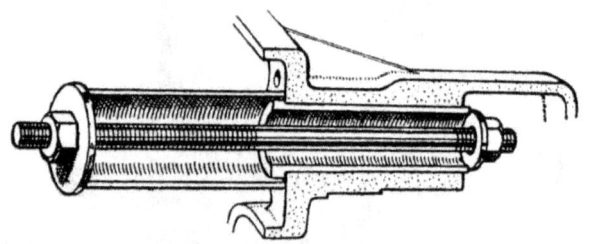

FIG. 67. EXTRACTING ROCKER BUSH (1938-47)

Norton Service Department is best qualified to tackle this job, and you should forward the timing cover and the corresponding crankcase half, or the complete crankcase, to Norton Motors, Ltd.

Dismantling the O.H.V. Rocker-box (1938–47). When the rocker-box has been removed from the engine, check the rocker assembly for wear and end float of the bushes and spindles. Remove the valve rocker-arm nut and washer, and remove the rocker arm by lightly tapping the arm off the spindle taper. Then withdraw the spindle and push-rod arm from the rocker-box. Next remove the push-rod arm.

There should be no perceptible end float in the rocker-spindle assembly. Excessive end float can be remedied by fitting shims supplied by Norton Motors, Ltd.

A worn rocker bush can be extracted in the manner shown in Fig. 67, which is self-explanatory. New bushes should be pressed in, or tapped home with a hammer and wooden block. After fitting a new bush, see that the necessary oil holes are drilled.

To detach the exhaust-valve lifter, remove the cable from the arm. Then take out the securing pin in the top of the rocker-box and withdraw the valve lifter, complete with the arm.

Should it be necessary to renew a rocker ball-end or a valve-rocker pad, it may readily be knocked out.

GENERAL MAINTENANCE

Dismantling Rocker-box on O.H.V. Engines (1948 Onwards). The rocker-box of a Model 18, 19R, 19S, ES2, or 50 engine is fairly readily stripped down after it has been removed from the cylinder head. To remove the rockers for inspection and perhaps rebushing, take off the rocker-box inspection cover and remove the rocker spindle nuts and washers. Then drift the rocker spindles out by using a soft-nosed punch applied to their threaded ends. Afterwards extract the rockers from the rocker-box, together with their washers and shims.

To remove the exhaust-valve lifter from the rocker-box, first remove the small securing screw and then withdraw the valve lifter. If renewal of the

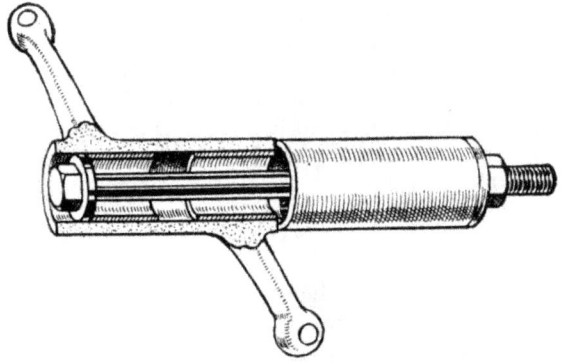

FIG. 68. EXTRACTING ROCKER BUSHES (1948 ONWARDS)

rocker ball-ends and pads is called for, drift these out from the rockers with a suitable punch. Where it is desired to rebush the rockers, the simple method of drawing them out suggested in Fig. 68 can be used. The bushes are a press fit.

Repairs to Rocker-box (1948 Onwards). If new rocker-ends are needed, press them into position. Make sure that the hole in the shank of the ball end registers with the oil hole drilled in the rocker arm. If new rocker bushes are required to be fitted, reverse the method of extraction indicated in Fig. 68. After pressing or drawing in new bushes, ream them both with a $\frac{9}{16}$ in. diameter reamer.

Assembling the Rocker-box. The exploded view of the upper part of the O.H.V. engine shown on page 87, indicates clearly the relative positions of the various parts comprising the rocker-box assembly. The steel shims on each side of the spring washer have the same Part No., but the thrust washer at the opposite end is considerably thicker.

To assemble each rocker in the rocker-box, obtain a steel bar of slightly smaller diameter than the large spindle hole and with a lead on one end.

Slip this bar into the hole sufficiently far to enable the shims and spring washer to be placed over it. Now thread the rocker carefully into position. To ensure that the rocker goes fully home, it may be necessary to withdraw the bar slightly. Centralize the washers as far as is possible. Then remove the bar and insert the rocker spindle which should first be oiled. With a soft-nosed punch tap the rocker spindle so that it partially enters the rocker.

Next, with a screwdriver inserted into the push-rod hole (and bearing on the rocker arm), compress the spring washer, and position the thrust washer. Until the rocker spindle is tapped farther home the pressure exerted by the spring washer will retain the thrust washer in position. If the thrust washer is not truly aligned and is pinched between the shoulder on the rocker spindle and the rocker-box itself, tap the opposite end of the rocker spindle once only in order to release the thrust washer.

Again compress the spring washer by means of the screwdriver. This should enable the thrust washer to become properly located. Now interpose some tin strip or the end of a steel rule between the thrust washer and the rocker-box and tap the rocker spindle right home. Afterwards remove the strip or rule and verify that the rocker moves freely. Finally replace the copper washer and dome nut. Tighten the latter securely.

Valve Guides. They are a driving fit in the cylinder head or cylinder barrel and, to remove, tap them out with a double-diameter drift. Removal, however, is only necessary if excessive clearance between the valves and guides has developed through wear. Use the above-mentioned drift to fit new guides or replace old ones. After fitting valve guides, it is generally necessary to true up the valve seats with a cutter to ensure that the seats and guides are in true alignment (*see also* Fig. 37).

Removing Engine from Cradle Frame. Complete removal of the engine from the cradle frame, used on all 1946 and later Nortons and some 1938-9 models, is advisable when undertaking a very thorough overhaul. This presents no great difficulty. First, remove the petrol tank (*see* page 73), take off the "Magdyno" (*see* page 102), and disconnect the exhaust-valve lifter cable. Then remove as a unit the Amal carburettor. If desired, this may be left attached to the control cables. With the "C" spanner provided in the tool kit, undo the locking ring (on O.H.V. models) which secures the exhaust pipe to the exhaust port. Remove completely the exhaust pipe and the silencer. By undoing the clip bolts and nuts, the exhaust pipe and silencer can be removed together, instead of separately.

Disconnect at the crankcase the delivery and return pipes leading to the oil tank. If the latter has not been drained, plug the end of the delivery pipe. Remove the oil-bath chain case, the engine sprocket, and also the clutch. Take off the front and rear engine plates, remove the engine cradle bolts, and lift the engine right out of the cradle frame.

GENERAL MAINTENANCE

Inspecting Connecting-rod Bearings. Both the big-end and the small-end bearings can be inspected for wear when the cylinder barrel is taken off the engine. To examine the condition of the big-end bearing, turn the flywheels until the big-end is at T.D.C. Then grip the connecting-rod with *both* hands, and push and pull it in a vertical direction. Be careful not to exert any side pressure, as some end float is permissible. A small amount of up-and-down movement is acceptable, but appreciable "rock" indicates excessive wear, and a new crankpin bearing is called for. This necessitates parting the crankcase halves and the dismantling of the flywheel assembly.

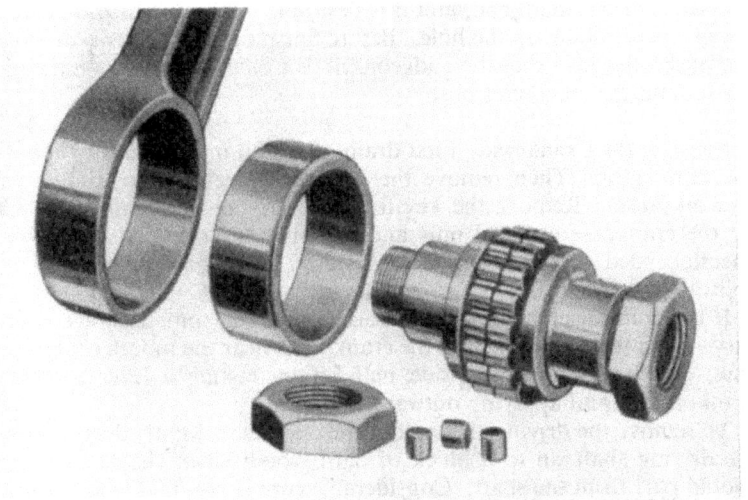

FIG. 69. THE STURDY BIG-END BEARING (ALL S.V. AND O.H.V.)

The former is a job which can be undertaken readily; but the latter, and the fitting of a new big-end bearing (and subsequent aligning of the flywheels), is a job best undertaken by the makers, who have the necessary jigs and tools available.

The complete flywheel assembly (or preferably the entire crankcase, stripped of parts not in need of attention) should be forwarded to the Service Department of Norton Motors, Ltd., or to an authorized Norton repairer. Those with some workshop facilities and experience can, however, tackle the job of renewing the small-end bush if this is found to be excessively worn. The gudgeon-pin itself is hard and is not likely to show much wear even after a very big mileage. It should be a good running fit in both the small-end bush and the piston bosses. Play can readily be detected by attempting to "rock" the pin in its bush. Obviously, if both the big-end and small-end bearings need attention, the whole of the work is best done by the makers, or expert mechanics.

Renewing Small-end Bush. To extract the worn bush from the small-end of the connecting rod, obtain a bolt about twice as long as the small-end bush. Fit a plain washer (with outside diameter less than that of the bush) to the head of the bolt. Then insert the bolt into the bush.

Fit over the screwed end of the bolt a piece of tube which has an inside diameter slightly greater than the outside diameter of the bush, and which is longer than the bush. Now fit a nut to the bolt, and to extract the bush, tighten the nut as required. Be careful not to strain the connecting-rod.

Prior to fitting a new small-end bush, ream its inside diameter to the gudgeon-pin diameter. This is necessary because the bush contracts when pressed into the small-end, and it is desirable to avoid removing excessive metal when trueing up the hole. Before finishing, drill the two oil holes in the bush. See also that the gudgeon-pin is a *running fit* in both the piston bosses and the small-end bush.

Splitting the Crankcase. First drain off all oil in the sump by removing the drain plug. Then remove the cylinder barrel, piston, timing gears, and oil pump. Remove the key from the driving-side mainshaft. Undo all the crankcase external nuts and tap out the bolts. Also remove the cheese-headed screws from the oil sump. It is now possible to begin splitting the crankcase.

If the crankcase halves do not readily separate, some leverage is necessary. Turn the flywheels until the crankpin is near the mouth of the crankcase, and lever the timing-side half off by resting a lever against the crankpin nut and applying outward leverage.

To remove the driving-side half of the crankcase, lightly drop the end of the driving shaft on to a block of hard wood, when the crankcase half should part from the shaft. Considerable care is required when fitting the flywheel assembly to the crankcase and bolting the two halves together. For this reason the author advocates that when big-end trouble develops, the complete flywheel *and* crankcase assembly be sent to the Norton Service Department at Bracebridge Street, Birmingham, 6, for their expert attention. If you have sufficient confidence, split the crankcase, forward the flywheel assembly only, and reassemble the crankcase yourself.

The Crankcase Bearings. These can be tapped out with suitable drifts, but the judicious application of heat to the bearing housings may in some instances be necessary. In view of the care required and the issues at stake, it is probably advisable for most Norton owners to entrust bearing renewal to Norton Motors, Ltd. If the big-end requires renewal, the remaining bearings should be closely examined.

Assembling the Crankcase. Fit the flywheel assembly temporarily into the crankcase, and secure the crankcase halves by fitting and tightening *all* bolts. Then check the flywheels for correct end float (0·005 in.). If end

GENERAL MAINTENANCE

float is found excessive, take out the flywheel assembly and fit pen-steel washers as required to both main shafts. To ensure central disposition of the flywheels in the crankcase, be sure to fit the same thickness of washers on each side. Replace the flywheel assembly, bolt up the crankcase, and again check the end float.

Next check that the connecting-rod is quite central in the crankcase, taking into account connecting-rod end float. Grip the base of the connecting-rod and push it towards the timing side as far as possible. Then measure the distance between the mouth of the crankcase and the end of the small-end bush on the timing side. Similarly push the connecting-rod hard over to the driving side and record the same measurement on this side. The difference between the two measurements should not exceed $\frac{1}{64}$ in. To make an adjustment for alignment, transfer pen-steel washers from one side to the other as required. After obtaining correct alignment, remove the flywheel assembly from the crankcase and proceed with the final assembly.

Oil the big-end and main-shaft bearings. Then smear some jointing compound or gold size on the two edges of the crankcase halves. Fit the flywheel assembly into the crankcase and bolt up the latter. Replace the timing gears and oil pump, also the timing cover (*see* page 107). After fitting the cylinder, etc., check the valve timing.

If a valve-guide lubricator has been removed from the crankcase of a S.V. engine, be sure to replace this. Screw the lubricator home and check that the oil holes point *towards the valve stems*. The bevelled side must face towards the cylinder.

Fitting Engine to Cradle Frame. Proceed in the reverse order of dismantling. Carefully lift the engine into the cradle, and insert both cradle bolts. Beginning at the rear engine plates, fit all bolts loosely and work round to the front engine-plate bolt. Afterwards tighten all securing nuts firmly. Complete the assembly by replacing the clutch, engine sprocket, oil-bath chain case, etc. Replace the Lucas "Magdyno" (*see* page 102) and time it correctly (*see* page 96). Finally reconnect the oil pipes, and fit the exhaust system, carburettor, and petrol tank.

THE TRANSMISSION

Clutch Adjustment. Nothing is more exasperating or inconvenient on a motor-cycle than clutch-slip. The cable adjustment should be adjusted until there is approximately $\frac{1}{8}$ in. of idle movement at the end of the clutch worm lever. It may be necessary to loosen the clutch-worm lever from the worm to find a more convenient operating position. The only parts of the clutch liable to wear are the friction plates, which are easily replaced. The clutch should be adjusted immediately any sign of slipping is felt, or if there is some "drag" present. The latter renders gear changing difficult, and the selection of neutral very uncertain.

When fitting up the control wire for the clutch, ease off the bends as much as possible to ensure long life and easy movement of the inner wire, and keep the cable greased where friction occurs.

To Adjust Clutch (Pre-1946). Lack of sufficient free movement in the clutch-worm lever with the control cable slackened off at the cable stop may be caused through the shoulder on the worm bearing on the face of the felt washer, this washer being held in place by a steel cap on which are machined two flats to take a spanner. The remedy is to release the steel cap a few threads. Always keep the clutch spring pressure-adjusters fully tightened.

To Adjust Clutch (1946 Onwards). The procedure for taking up slack in the clutch cable is to loosen the lock-nut and then turn the adjuster for the cable as required. Should further cable adjustment be impossible or result in the clutch-worm lever assuming an unfavourable position, effect an adjustment by means of the worm lever. This lever is accessible on removing the two screws securing the oval cover (*see* Fig. 76) to the gearbox outer cover. The oval cover is incidentally a good fit in the outer cover and on later models forms an outrigger bearing for the clutch operating-worm. On 1946 models the cover is of the sprung-in type.

If the oval cover referred to above is tight, tap round it gently until the ends stand away from the outer cover and provide two lips into which suitable levers may be inserted. Be careful not to use excessive force.

To make a worm-lever adjustment, slacken the cable adjuster right down and then turn the lever on the shank of the worm after releasing the pinch bolt and while holding the shank by means of the slot machined across its end. Turn the clutch-worm lever *anti-clockwise* until it is about 45 degrees below the horizontal. Then effect the necessary cable adjustment and verify that the angle between the cable and worm lever is approximately a right-angle with the clutch fully disengaged. No adjustment of the clutch-spring pressure is provided, and the clutch-spring pins must be kept screwed fully home.

Gearbox Lubrication. *See* page 35.

Primary Chain Adjustment. The chain is automatically lubricated and enclosed in an oil-bath chain case; stretching takes considerably longer than is the case with the secondary chain, which is much more exposed to harmful influences. However, it will stretch in time, and it must be retensioned correctly. The chain should be adjusted and kept adjusted, so that it can be given midway by pressure with the fingers a total and maximum deflection* of roughly $\frac{3}{8}$ in. Adjustment is effected by slackening the

* Always check the tension of a chain with the chain in various positions, and adjust with the chain in its tightest position.

GENERAL MAINTENANCE

top and bottom gearbox-bolts, and turning the adjuster on the offside of the machine clockwise until the correct tension is arrived at. Retighten the two gearbox bolts and retension the secondary chain.

Secondary Chain Adjustment. The chain requires to be tensioned at regular intervals, depending upon the mileage of the machine and how the rider has lubricated the chain (*see* page 38).

FIG. 70. THE SECONDARY-CHAIN ADJUSTMENT ON SPRING FRAME NORTONS (PRE-1956)

On the rigid-frame models adjuster screws are used instead of drawbolts, and these bear on the front side of the spindle.
- A. Hub-spindle nut.
- B. Drawbolt-adjuster nut.
- C. Drawbolt-adjuster lock-nut.
- D. Drawbolt.
- E. Brake-rod adjuster nut.

To retension the secondary chain, first unscrew the wing-nut (E, Fig. 70) on the rear-brake rod and slightly loosen the two hub-spindle nuts A.

Now on rigid-frame models loosen the two adjuster screw lock-nuts, being careful not to disturb the adjuster screws themselves. Turn both adjuster screws clockwise *the same amount* until the total chain movement on deflecting the lower chain run midway between the sprockets is approximately $\frac{1}{2}-\frac{3}{4}$ in.

On pre-1956 spring-frame models, after slackening the rear-brake adjuster nut and the hub-spindle nuts, adjust the tension of the chain in the following manner. Referring to Fig. 70, slacken the two drawbolt-adjuster lock-nuts C and with the appropriate spanner turn both drawbolt-adjuster nuts B clockwise *the same amount* until the total chain movement (with the chain in its tightest position) midway between the sprockets on the lower run is approximately $\frac{3}{4}$ in. *with the weight of the machine on the rear wheel*.

On 1956 spring-frame models unscrew the rear-brake adjuster nut, loosen both spindle nuts, slacken the adjuster screw lock-nuts, and turn the adjuster screws *anti-clockwise* the same amount until the chain tension is correct (*see* previous paragraph).

Tighten the two small lock-nuts and the hub-spindle nuts securely, and check that the wheel alignment has not been upset during the above chain adjustment (*see* page 135). Also readjust the rear brake (*see* page 133).

Chain Stretch. A simple check for chain stretch is to remove the chain from the machine, lay it on a flat surface, and stretch it to its full extent. Measure 24 pitches between bearing-pin centres. In the event of the chain showing more than one-quarter of an inch per foot elongation, renew the chain.

The Spring Link. Always reconnect a chain so that the *closed* end of the spring link faces the direction of chain travel. This is most important.

To Remove Oil-bath Cover (1938–9). Dismantling the clutch on the 1938–9 models necessitates detaching the chain-case cover. To do this, disconnect the brake pedal and also the exhaust pipe (if one is fitted on the near side). Then remove the footrest and take off the large nut screwed on the footrest tube. Removal of this nut enables the cover to be withdrawn, exposing the primary chain and clutch (Fig. 71). When doing this be careful to ease off the cover equally all round and not to damage in any way the oil-sealing rubber band. When replacing the cover it is important to avoid using excessive force while tightening the footrest-tube nut. This should only be done up tight enough to hold the cover firmly and evenly in contact with the rubber band.

To Dismantle the Clutch (1938–9). Remove the clutch-spring screws and take out the springs and spring boxes. Next remove the spring circlip surmounting the clutch body by inserting a screwdriver beneath the spring and lifting it from its retaining groove. The plates can now be withdrawn, and note the order in which they are fitted to ensure correct replacement.

To Dismantle Vane Type Shock-absorber (1938–9). To dismantle the vane type shock-absorber (Fig. 71) fitted for 1938–9, unscrew the three

GENERAL MAINTENANCE

countersunk-head screws holding the retaining plate to the outside of the clutch body. It is then possible to withdraw the rubbers unless they have been in use a long time and have become stuck, in which case a penknife should be used to free them from the metal vanes.

To Remove Oil-bath (1946 Onwards). Remove the footrests, footrest rod, and the rear-brake pedal. Then remove the large nut which secures

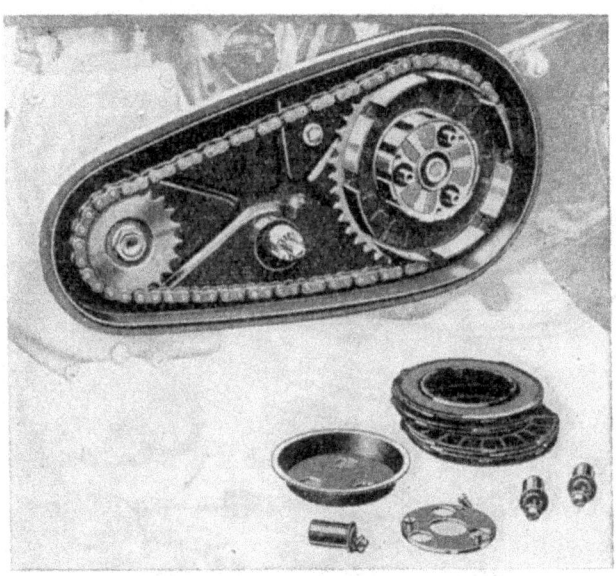

FIG. 71. SHOWING OIL-BATH CHAIN CASE WITH COVER REMOVED AND CLUTCH DISMANTLED

Note the vane-type rubber shock-absorber incorporated in the clutch body (*see also* Fig. 72).

the outer portion of the oil-bath, and detach the latter. Next remove the clutch-spring screws, the clutch springs, and the cups. Each of these members is in triplicate. Also remove the clutch outer-plate, the clutch thrust-pin, and the clutch retaining-nut. While unscrewing this nut, depress the foot change until first gear is obtained and grip the rear wheel. After removing the retaining nut, withdraw the clutch body; to do this a special tool is available if necessary (*see* page 62).

With a claw-type extractor, proceed to remove the engine sprocket. Having done this, remove together the engine sprocket, clutch, and primary chain. Finally remove the inner portion of the oil-bath, which is secured by two bolts and two nuts. The inner portion of the oil-bath is secured to the crankcase by a bolt, to the engine plate by a nut, to the secondary-chain guard by a bolt, and to the gearbox pivot-bolt by a nut.

To Replace Oil-bath (1946 Onwards). Assemble it in the reverse order to that used for removal. Inspect the rubber washer fitted to the flange of the inner portion. This constitutes the oil seal, and must be in sound condition to prevent oil leakage. After assembly is completed, replenish

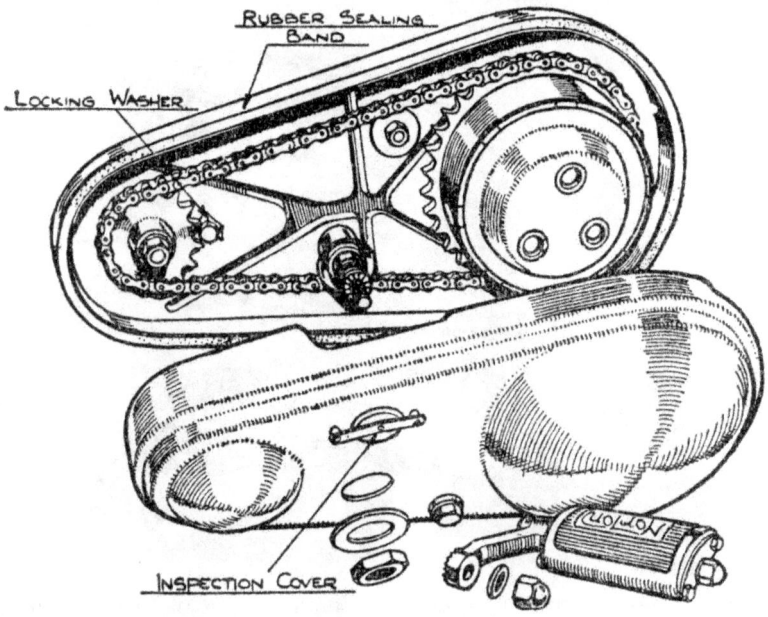

Fig. 72. Oil-bath Chain Case with Cover Removed (1946 Onwards)

the oil-bath with engine oil (*see* page 36) to the level of the plug situated close to the bottom of the outer portion of the oil-bath.

Dismantling Clutch (1946 Onwards). First remove the outer portion of the oil-bath. Also remove the clutch body (*see* appropriate instructions). If it is desired to inspect the driving slots in the clutch sprocket, it is necessary to remove the steel band which is pressed round the clutch sprocket. But if it is the rider's intention to dismantle the clutch plates only, it is permissible to leave this band in position. Its function, incidentally, is to prevent excessive oil getting on the plates.

To remove the clutch plates, detach the circlip which holds the plates on to the clutch body and withdraw the plates. It will be observed that they comprise six plain steel plates, and five steel plates with Ferodo inserts. Now remove the clutch sprocket.

Referring to Fig. 73, grip an old gearbox main-axle (if to hand) between the jaws of a vice, with the splined end above the jaws, and fit the clutch body to the axle. Remove all three screws holding the front cover-plate. Now remove the clutch cover-plate and the shock-absorber rubbers (*see*

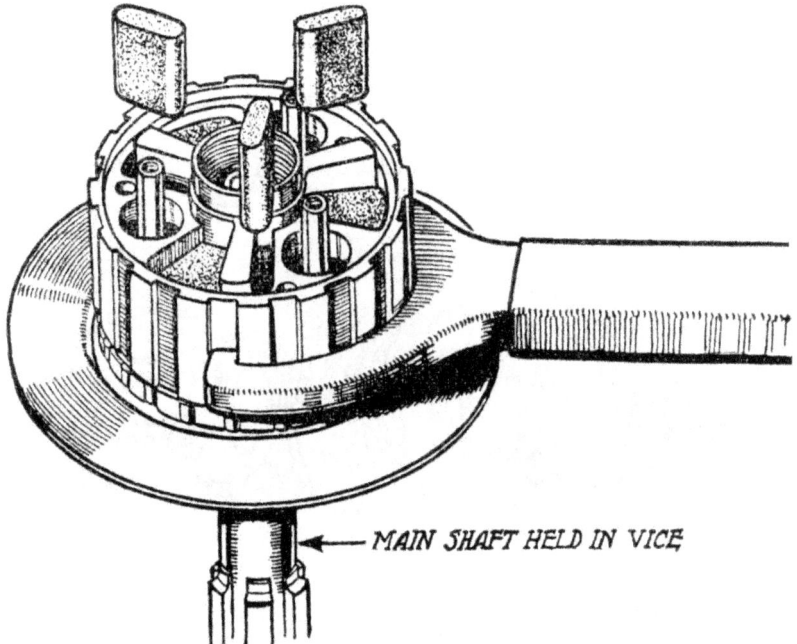

Fig. 73. Removing Shock-absorber Rubbers from Clutch Body

Fig. 73). Remove the rubbers with a large "C" spanner. Place the spanner over the body so as to engage the splines as illustrated. Compress the large rubbers while removing the smaller ones. The length of the spanner should be such that the load can be taken by the operator's thighs, while both hands are free to remove the shock-absorber rubbers. A good substitute for a "C" spanner is an old plain steel clutch-plate with handle attached. To remove the large and smaller rubbers, it is advisable to use a small, sharp-pointed tool.

Remove the clutch body from the axle and replace in the reverse position. Then remove the three nuts from the studs of the back-cover plate. Then separate the back plate, roller race, back cover, and clutch body.

Inspecting Clutch Parts (1946 Onwards). When occasion is had to strip down the clutch (see Fig. 74), during a complete overhaul, make a close inspection of the various components. Visually inspect the inserts in each friction plate. They must be proud of the steel plate in which they are fitted. If new inserts are fitted, see that they are all level and flat, and all contact the adjacent plain steel-plates. The fitting of a few new inserts separately is bad practice.

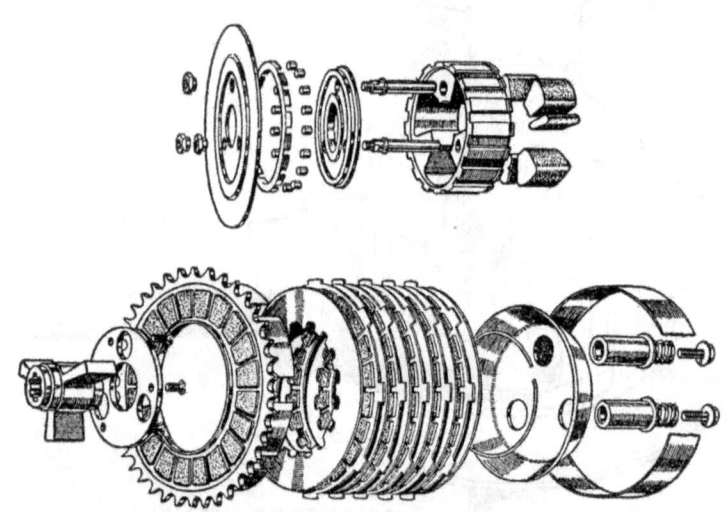

FIG. 74. EXPLODED VIEW OF NORTON MULTI-PLATE CLUTCH (1946 ONWARDS)

The upper components should be regarded as being in line with and to the left of the lower members.

Look for wear on the drive of the plates. The drive of the plain steel-plates is taken on the inside circumference, but that for the friction-insert plates is taken on the outside circumference.

The splines on the clutch centre and the corresponding splines on the plain steel-plates seldom show signs of wear, but this does not necessarily apply to the tongues on the friction-insert plates. Sometimes these tongues wear, and occasionally they bite into the driven part of the combined sprocket and casing. Wear of this nature interferes with smooth clutch action. The remedy is to file or grind the tongues on the plates square, and also the edge of the driven part of the sprocket. The only ill effect will be some slight backlash in the control, which does not matter.

Inspect the plain steel-plates for signs of roughness, especially the back plate. Verify the condition of the bearing rollers, race, and cage. See if the back-cover plate is worn by the clutch centre. Also inspect the shock-absorber rubbers for evidence of cracking or softening.

Assembling Clutch (1946 Onwards). Assemble the clutch body cover-plate to the body. Check that the mating holes are in alignment and the spring studs an easy fit. Replace the clutch-body centre and fit the large shock-absorber rubbers. Compress these and fit the smaller ones. Replace the clutch-body front cover and tighten the screws. Fit the roller race on to the back-cover plate and replace the back-plate spring studs. Fit nuts to the studs and tighten them, finally locking the nuts with a centre-punch. Test the roller race for freeness on its track.

Replace the steel band on the sprocket, making sure that the latter does not become distorted. Check all clutch plates for free movement and fit the clutch sprocket to the body. Rotate the sprocket on the race to verify free running. Next assemble the clutch plates on the sprocket and body. The correct order of fitting is: plain steel; inserts; plain, etc. The bevelled edges of the plates must be *towards* the sprocket. Turn the sprocket to see whether the plates are free.

Fit the plate retaining-circlip and assemble the clutch to the gearbox main-shaft. Replace the clutch thrust-pin, clutch outer plate, spring cups, springs, and spring pins. Tighten the latter *fully*, and then complete the assembly by replacing the outer portion of the oil-bath.

To Remove Gearbox Outer Cover (1946 Onwards). First remove the kick-starter crank by loosening the pinch-bolt and pulling the crank off. Next detach the foot gear-change indicator by unscrewing the centre bolt from the spindle. Also remove the gear-change lever by unscrewing its pinch-bolt and pulling the lever off the shaft splines. Now remove all the cheese-headed screws which secure the gearbox outer cover and very carefully withdraw the cover. Be careful not to tear the paper washer used for the joint. If this is damaged during removal, renew it at once. Should the joint be difficult to break, do not attempt to prise the cover off, but apply a punch at the extremities where the outer cover overhangs the inner cover (on all recent gearboxes).

Note that the removal of the outer cover necessarily involves the loss of some oil which must be replenished through the clutch-worm inspection hole until oil begins to drip from the level-plug hole which is normally plugged by the square-headed level plug situated to the rear of and on the same level as the kick-starter crank. When the outer cover is replaced, tighten all the cheese-headed securing screws lightly and then firmly in opposite pairs.

Dismantling the Foot Gear-change (1946-9). First remove the gearbox outer cover, and remove the return-spring cover plate, which is secured by two nuts. Detach the return spring, and remove the pawl carrier by sliding it off the ratchet plate spindle, complete with the pawls and pawl spring.

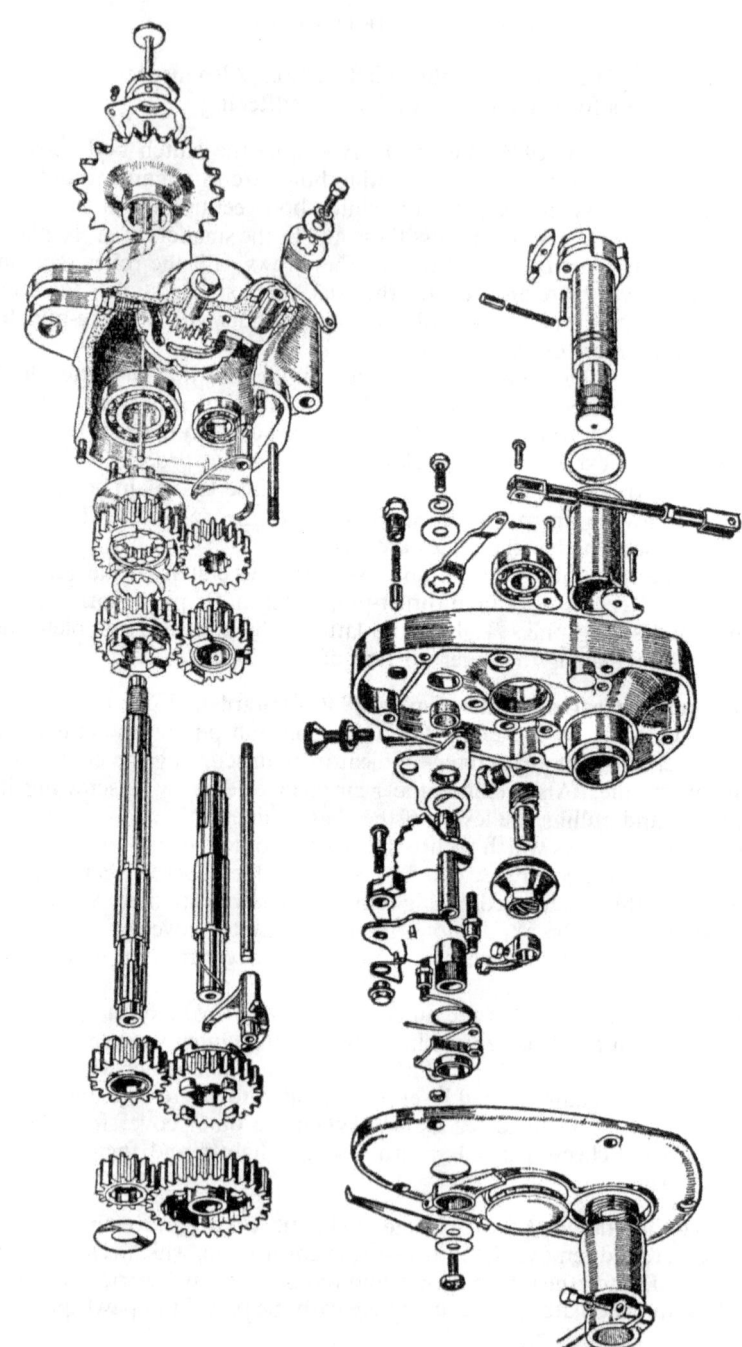

FIG. 75. EXPLODED VIEW OF NORTON GEARBOX (1946–9)

GENERAL MAINTENANCE

Remove the ratchet lever. A bolt with a spring and plain washer secures the lever to the back of the control box. Now remove the ratchet plate, which has a plain steel-washer behind it. Remove the ratchet plunger at the back of the control box by removing the domed nut and releasing the plunger and spring. Remove the two nuts at the back of the box locking the pawl-carrier stop studs.

Remove the pawl-carrier stop studs and also the cam plate. Then remove the pawls from the pawl carrier by removing the sleeve nut on the pawl pin. Hold the end of the pawl pin with a screwdriver while unscrewing the nut. The pawls and return spring are now quite free.

Assembling the Foot Gear-change (1946-9). Assemble the spring and pawls to the pawl carrier. See that the pawls are free to move after tightening the nut. Position the cam plate and fit the two carrier-stops securing the cam plate. Fit the carrier-stop stud lock-nuts at the back of the box and fit the ratchet plate. Also fit the splined end of the spindle through the bush in the cam plate, and the steel washer between the ratchet and box. Assemble the felt washer on to the splined end of the shaft and into the boss on the back of the control box. With fourth gear engaged, fit the ratchet lever as high as possible.

Fit the remaining bolt and washers. See that the spring washer is next to the bolt head. Assemble the plunger and spring. Replace the pawl carrier, complete with pawls. The latter may be sprung into position with the assistance of a screwdriver. Fit the cover for the return spring, the two nuts, and grease as required. Replace the outer cover, gear-change lever, and indicator. Finally fit the kick-starter crank.

Dismantling the Foot Gear-change (1950 Onwards). Remove the gearbox outer-cover as previously described. This exposes to view the positive foot gear-change mechanism. To dismantle the mechanism, remove the two nuts which secure the U-section outer plate and withdraw this plate and then the lever return-spring, the pawl carrier, and the ratchet plate, A spacing shim will be found behind the latter. It is very improbable that the cam plate secured behind the shoulders of the two studs carrying the assembly will ever require to be removed, but no difficulty should be experienced if removal does become necessary.

After dismantling the foot gear-change mechanism, carefully inspect all parts for wear which is likely to cause lost movement when the foot gear-change is in use. Scrutinize particularly carefully the spindle bushes in both covers, the ends of the pawls and the pawl pin. Renew all appreciably worn parts and proceed to reassemble the foot gear-change mechanism as described below.

Assembling the Foot Gear-change Mechanism (1950 Onwards). First verify that the two studs which carry the assembly are quite secure, and

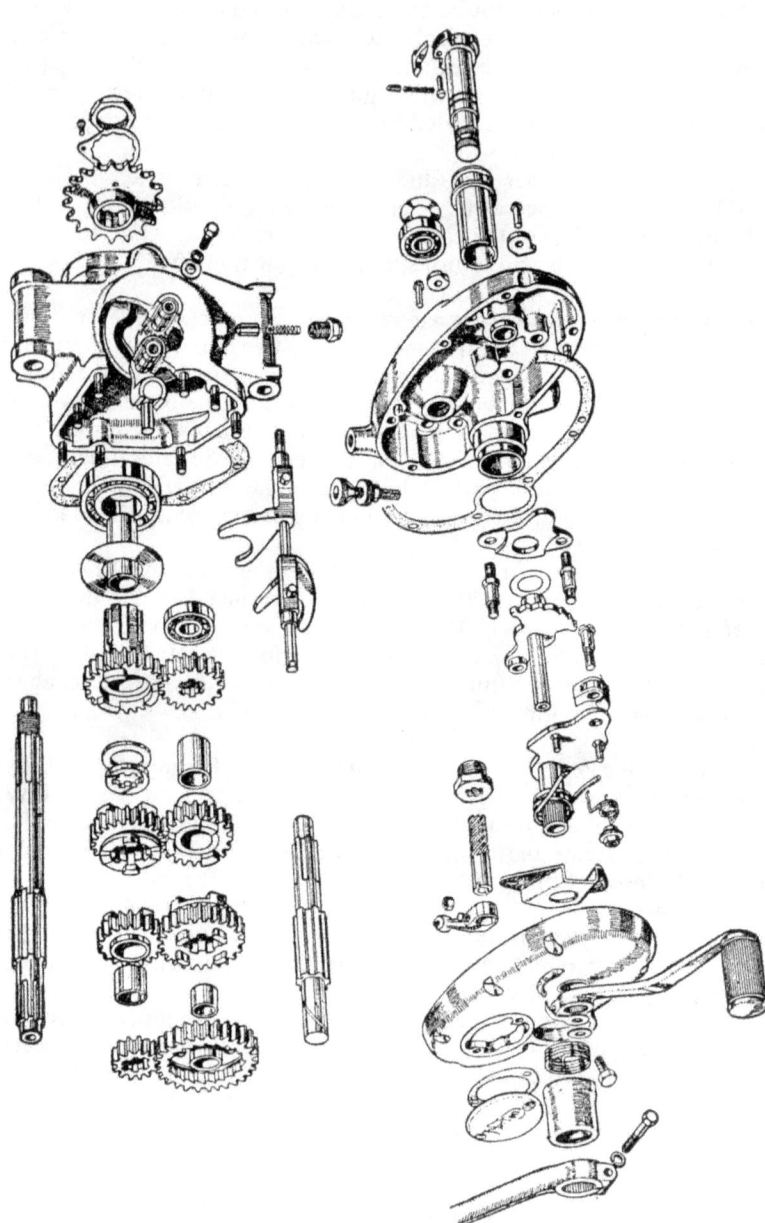

Fig. 76. Exploded View of Norton Gearbox 1950 Onwards

slip the spacing shim on the short shaft of the ratchet plate. Do not forget to insert the knuckle-pin (visible through the aperture in the inner cover) into the hole in the ratchet-plate arm when the ratchet plate is being assembled. While pushing home the pawl carrier, it is necessary to spread the pawls to enter the ratchet teeth.

To Remove Gearbox from Frame (1946–9). Remove the gearbox outer-cover and also release the clutch cable from the clutch arm. Unscrew the cable adjuster from the inner cover. Next remove the outer portion of the oil-bath, the clutch, and the engine sprocket (*see* page 117). Now remove the inner portion of the oil-bath (*see* page 117), the secondary-chain guard (secured at the rear by a nut and bolt), and the secondary chain. Also remove the rear wheel (*see* pages 127–9).

Remove the tool box (secured by three bolts), and detach the rear mudguard (secured by six bolts). Remove the large hexagon nut from the gearbox top-bolt and also the two bolts securing the gearbox adjuster-plate. Unscrew the adjuster bolt from the gearbox bolt and withdraw the gearbox top-bolt. Finally remove the gearbox bottom-nut and bolt, and lift the gearbox out of the frame.

To Remove Gearbox from Frame (1950 Onwards). Remove the gearbox outer-cover (*see* page 121). Also release the clutch control-cable from its operating arm by rotating the worm with a large screwdriver. Detach the cable adjuster from the inner cover. Now remove the oil-bath outer portion, the clutch, and engine sprocket (*see* page 117). Removal of the nut securing the engine sprocket is facilitated by engaging bottom gear and getting someone to hold the rear wheel while the nut is being spannered.

Remove the inner portion of the oil-bath (*see* page 117), the secondary-chain guard, and the secondary chain. Also remove the nut and adjuster bolt from the off-side of the gearbox top-bolt and extract the bolt from the near-side. Detach the spring from the prop stand, and also the nut from the off-side of the gearbox bottom-bolt. Remove the nut and tap out the bolt. Now swing the gearbox round in an anti-clockwise direction and lift it out of the frame on the off-side.

Gearbox Overhaul. Provided that the gearbox is kept properly topped-up with engine oil (*see* page 35) and reasonable care is taken when gear changing, a gearbox overhaul should not be necessary until a very big mileage has been covered. If the gearbox eventually becomes noisy and gear changing difficult, it is advisable to remove the gearbox from the frame (*see* above notes) and have it thoroughly overhauled by the makers or a reputable repairer. As gearbox overhaul is rather beyond the average Norton owner, appropriate dismantling, inspection, and assembling instructions are not included in this section. Exploded views of the 1946–9 and 1950 and later gearboxes, however, are shown in Figs. 75 and 76. For detailed instructions, you are referred to those given in the official Norton instruction book issued with each new machine.

WHEELS, BRAKES, AND TYRES

No Adjustment for Wheel Bearings. No adjustment is necessary or provided for the journal-type bearings fitted to the wheel hubs of 1938–56 Norton models.

To Remove Quickly-detachable Rear Wheel (1938–9). Withdraw the hub spindle, distance-piece and, in the case of some models, the plated

Fig. 77. Removing Quickly-detachable Rear Wheel (1938–9)

cover from the off-side of the machine. This cover is held in position by a concealed claw-spring, and it is only necessary to grip the cover under the hands and afterwards proceed to pull it away from the hub. If it appears to be unduly tight, insert a screwdriver or any handy instrument between the cover and the hub to force the cover off the hub. Remove the three sleeve-nuts which secure the hub to the brake drum. The wheel may now be withdrawn from the brake drum and readily detached, leaving the drum and chain sprocket in position. The rear of the mudguard is detachable.

To Remove Front Wheel 1938–9. Disconnect the cable "U" piece from the brake lever, slacken both spindle nuts and lift the wheel out. If it is desired to remove the brake drum, unscrew the three sleeve-nuts which are identical to those used on the rear wheel.

GENERAL MAINTENANCE

To Remove Sidecar Wheel. In order to detach the sidecar wheel all that is necessary is to withdraw the hub spindle and lift the wheel out.

To Remove Wheel Bearings (1938–9). Detach the locking ring on the off-side of the hub with a peg spanner or punch. Then tap out from the opposite side the inner sleeve on which the inside races of the bearings are fitted. Tap out the other bearing with a suitable drift.

Removing Front Wheel (Telescopic Forks). Place the Norton on both stands and disconnect the front-brake cable from the cam lever. Also disconnect the cable adjuster from the brake plate. Remove the off-side wheel-spindle nut, and loosen the pinch-bolt in the near-side fork end. With the left hand, support the front wheel and withdraw the spindle, using a tommy-bar inserted through the hole in the spindle head.

Fitting Front Wheel (Telescopic Forks). Follow the reverse order of dismantling. The spindle should be inserted from the near-side. After tightening the spindle nut, lock the pinch-bolt in the near-side fork end.

Removing Rear Wheel (Rigid Frame, 1946–55). Place the machine on the rear stand, and roll back the rubber tube on the lead of the rear lamp (pre-1953), so as to expose the brass connexion. Break the wire by parting the connector. On 1953 and later models disconnect the stop-tail lamp leads by pulling the cable either side of the rubber-covered snap connector behind the rear number plate. Then remove the rear mudguard tail-piece by taking out the two bolts which secure it to the main portion of the mudguard, also the two bolts at the bottom of the tail-piece holding the stays.

Detach the speedometer driving cable. Remove the wheel spindle, distance piece, and speedometer driving box. Next remove the nuts from the hub studs and draw the wheel clear of the three studs, and the wheel will come right away, leaving the brake drum in position.

The procedure for removing the rear wheel, complete with brake drum, is to remove the mudguard tail-piece, disconnect the secondary chain, remove the anchorage bolt securing the brake anchorage arm to the frame, remove the brake-rod adjuster nut, loosen the wheel-spindle nuts, and then ease the wheel out of the frame fork-ends.

Fitting Rear Wheel (Rigid Frame, 1946–55). Proceed in the reverse order of dismantling. Be careful to see that the wheel spindle is hard up against the secondary-chain adjusters. See that the chain spring-link has the *closed* end facing the direction of chain movement. Afterwards verify the adjustment of the rear brake and chain tension ($\frac{1}{2}$ in.–$\frac{3}{4}$ in.).

Removing Rear Wheel (Spring Frame, 1946–52). After placing the machine on the rear stand, disconnect the rear lamp as previously described for the rigid-frame models. Then remove the tail portion of the rear mudguard by removing the two bolts securing it to the main portion of the mudguard, and the two bolts holding the stays at the bottom of the tailpiece. Take off the adjuster nut from the brake rod and disconnect the speedometer drive. Slacken both rear-wheel spindle nuts and ease the rear wheel out of the fork ends.

Replacing Rear Wheel (Spring Frame, 1946–52). First verify that the spring frame fork-ends are lying reasonably parallel to each other. Then position the rear wheel. Ensure that the adjusting stirrup ears are flat against the sides of the fork end and that the cupped adjuster-washer is located on the small shoulder at the open end of the fork-end slot. Check that the anchor plate on the brake plate enters the slot on the inside of the near-side fork-end.

Replace the secondary chain (with closed end facing direction of travel), and tension it with the chain adjusters until there is about $\frac{3}{4}$ in. up-and-down movement midway between the chain sprockets. This adjustment *must* be obtained on spring-frame models with the weight of the motorcycle resting on the rear wheel. Finally adjust the rear brake and re-connect the speedometer drive.

Removing Rear Wheel (Spring Frame, 1953–55). On the 1953 and later Model ES2 and 19S Nortons with "swinging arm" rear suspension, the rear wheel is of the quickly-detachable type, identical to that used on the 1946–54 rigid-frame Model 18 Norton.

The rear mudguard has a hinged tail-piece to facilitate rear wheel removal which should be effected as already described for the rigid-frame models (1946–55), after lifting the hinged tail-piece.

To lift the hinged tail-piece, disconnect the stop-tail lamp wiring (*see* page 127) and then remove the end bolt from each side lifting-handle, when the tail-piece can be readily lifted.

Replacing Rear Wheel (Spring Frame, 1953–5). To replace the quickly-detachable rear wheel on Model ES2 or 19S with "swinging arm" rear suspension, reverse the procedure used for removing the wheel. When the wheel is replaced in the fork-ends, see that the hub spindle is hard up against the chain adjusters. When replacing the chain spring-link always verify that its *closed* end faces the direction of chain motion, and check that the tension of the chain (*see* page 116) is correct if the chain drawbolt-adjuster nuts (*B*, Fig. 70) have been disturbed. In this case, also verify that both wheels are in true alignment, and check the adjustment of the rear-brake pedal (*see* page 133).

Tighten both wheel-spindle nuts firmly and also connect up securely the

GENERAL MAINTENANCE   129

speedometer driving-cable. Finally tighten down the hinged tail-piece of the rear mudguard and see that the stop-tail lamp leads are properly reconnected with the snap connector.

Removing Rear Wheel (Spring Frame, 1956). On the 1956 Models ES2, 19S, and 50 with full-width light-alloy rear hubs and "swinging arm" rear suspension, a quickly-detachable rear wheel is provided. This can be readily removed as described below.

First place the machine on its centre stand and disconnect the tail and stop-light leads by pulling each cable either side of the rubber-covered snap-on connector located behind the rear number plate. Next remove the end bolt from each side lifting-handle. This enables the mudguard hinged tail-piece to be readily lifted when the rear wheel is withdrawn.

Now remove the three rubber plugs from the end of the wheel hub, thereby exposing the sleeve-nuts which retain the wheel. With a suitable box spanner remove the sleeve nuts. Also remove the rear wheel spindle and distance-piece. Then withdraw the rear wheel from the retaining studs, leaving the rear-brake drum and the secondary chain undisturbed.

If it is desired to remove the rear wheel together with the brake drum, disconnect the secondary chain and remove the chain guard. Also remove the knurled adjuster-nut on the end of the brake rod, disconnect the brake torque arm from the frame, and disconnect the speedometer drive. Then release the wheel spindle and nut from the near-side stub axle so as to enable the rear wheel to be slid along the adjusting slots and withdrawn.

Replacing Rear Wheel (Spring Frame, 1956). Replace the wheel in the reverse order of dismantling. Do not forget to fit the spring link on the chain with the open end facing *away from* the direction of chain movement. Also check that the chain adjuster-plates are correctly seated, and that the chain is tensioned so that there is about $\frac{3}{4}$ in. slackness (total up-and-down movement) in the centre of the chain lower run, with the chain in its tightest position and with the weight of the machine resting on the wheels. Check the rear brake adjustment, and if necessary, wheel alignment.

Dismantling Rear Hub (Rigid Frame, 1946–55). First remove the rear wheel. Then remove (*see* Fig. 78) in this order: the locking ring, felt washer, and distance-piece, from the plain side of the hub. Drift out the inner sleeve. This will simultaneously detach the single-row bearing. Knock out with a suitable punch the bearing in the brake side of the hub, together with the peened-in washer, felt washer, and pen-steel washer.

Dismantling Rear Hub (Spring Frame, 1946–52). Remove the complete rear wheel assembly (*see* page 128). Take off the wheel-spindle nuts, the adjusting stirrups, the brake plate, speedometer driving-box, and the distance-pieces. Next remove from the plain side of the hub the locking

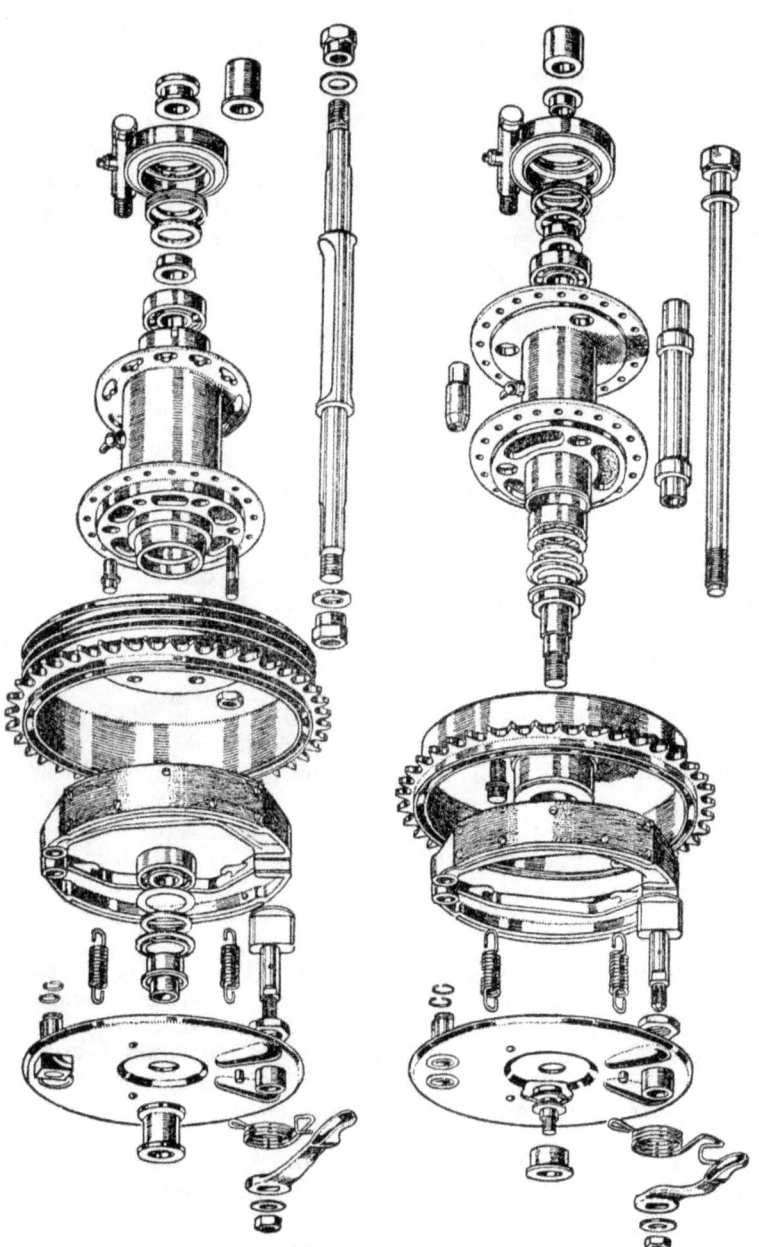

Fig. 78. Exploded Views of Rear Hub and Brake Assemblies

Above is shown the arrangement on 1946–52 spring-frame models, and below the arrangement on rigid-frame models (1946–55) and spring frame models (1953–55).

ring for the ball race. Detach the distance-piece and felt washer. Drive out the spindle, bringing with it the single-row bearing fitted to the plain side of the hub. Then drift out the remaining bearing along with the peened-in washer, and the felt and pen-steel washers which are fitted into the brake-drum side of the hub. If necessary, separate the hub and brake drum. Assemble the rear hub in the reverse order to that given above. Pack the bearings with grease.

Dismantling Rear Hub (Spring Frame, 1953 Onwards). Follow the instructions previously given for dismantling the rear hub on rigid-frame models (1946–55). Fig. 78 (lower sketch) shows an exploded view of the 1953–5 quickly-detachable wheel hub assembly.

Dismantling Front Hub (1946 Onwards). Remove the front wheel after placing the machine on both stands. Detach the brake plate, and its inner and outer distance-pieces. Remove the locking ring, felt washer, and distance-piece from the opposite side of the hub. Then, with a suitable punch, drive the bearing in the brake side farther into the hub, until the single-row bearing comes away. Take out the distance tube and from the same side of the hub, drift out the remaining bearing. The peened-in washer, felt washer, and pen-steel washer will come off with this bearing.

Assembling Rear Hub (Rigid Frame, 1946–55). Pack the bearings thoroughly with grease and fit the single-row bearing to the screwed side of the hub. Then fit the inner sleeve, the long end into the single-row bearing. Next replace the distance-piece, felt washer, and locking ring. Tighten the latter. Now press into position the double-row bearing and replace in this order: the pen-steel washer, the felt washer, and the dished washer. Rivet the latter lightly into place.

Assembling Rear Hub (Spring Frame, 1953 Onwards). The assembly procedure is the same as that just described for assembling the rear hub on rigid frame models (1946–55). An exploded view of the 1953–5 hub assembly is shown in Fig. 78 (lower sketch).

Assembling Front Hub (1946 Onwards). Lubricate the bearings by thoroughly packing them with grease. Press into position the single-row bearing, and then fit the distance-piece (with collar abutting the bearing), felt washer, and locking ring. Tighten the latter. Insert through the brake side of the hub the distance tube. See that it beds home against the bearing just fitted. Now press the double-row bearing into place, and fit the pen-steel washer and the felt washer. Afterwards rivet lightly the remaining washer into the recess provided.

Dismantling Brakes (1946 Onwards). First remove the brake plate from the brake drum. Detach the brake lever return-spring from the lever.

Then remove the nut and washer from the cam spindle. Also remove the brake lever. Remove the cam and its spindle from the bush in the brake plate. Tap the spindle end lightly until the cam clears the shoes. Take off the shoe return-springs and (on 1946–54 models) remove the circlips which secure the shoes to the pivot pins. On 1955 and later models remove the small pin from the end of each pivot pin and lift off the pivot pin tie-plate. Now remove the brake shoes. After removing the nut holding the cam-spindle bush to the brake plate, remove the bush.

Assembling Brakes (1946 Onwards). Proceed in the following manner. Fit the cam-spindle bush to the brake plate. Then fit the brake shoes and

FIG. 79. SHOWING THE REAR BRAKE ANCHOR-PLATE WITH SHOES IN POSITION AND THE QUICKLY-DETACHABLE REAR WHEEL HUB (PRE-1956)

smear a little oil on the pivot pins. Fit *one* shoe to the pivot pin. Then fit the spring (near the pin) to the shoe just fitted. Hold the second shoe close to that already fitted and attach the spring, stretch it, and fit the second shoe to the pivot pin. Now fit the second spring to both brake shoes. Fit the cam spindle to the plate. Separate the shoes with a suitable tool, such as a screwdriver, and allow the cam to pass the ends of the shoes.

Fit (on 1946–54 models) new circlips to both pivot pins, and assembly is complete. To facilitate the fitting of the circlips, it is advisable to employ a piece of rod (same diameter as the pivot pin) and a piece of tube to fit over the rod. Fit each circlip to the rod, and insert the tube over the rod. Place the rod at the end of the pivot pin, and then tap the end of the tube with a hammer. This will force the circlip on to the pin and into the groove.

GENERAL MAINTENANCE

On 1955 and later models, fit the tie-plate over the shoulders on the pivot pins, and fit and tighten both the pins.

Adjusting the Brakes. If the brakes are used too frequently and heavily, the friction linings are apt to wear, and adjustment becomes necessary.

In the case of the rear internal-expanding brake (*see* Fig. 79), there are two separate adjustments.

In addition to provision for taking up lining wear, an independent adjustment is provided for altering the angle of the brake-pedal lever; thus

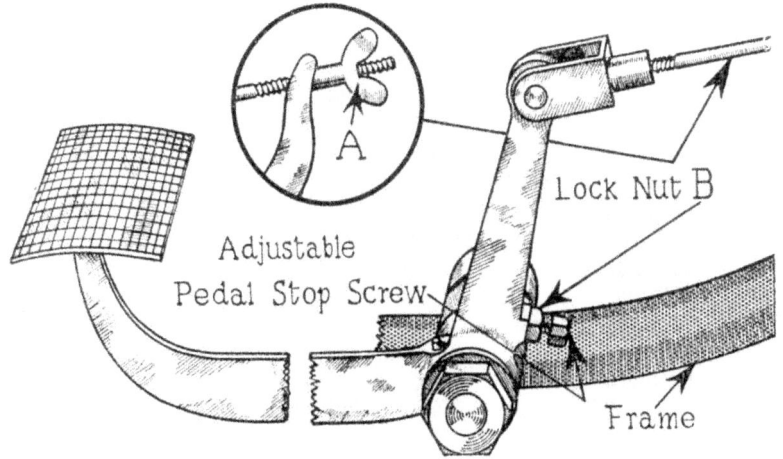

FIG. 80. THE DUAL ADJUSTMENT FOR THE REAR BRAKE
Comprising an adjustable pedal stop and a wing-nut *A* for adjusting the length of the brake-rod. On 1946–56 models the cam-operating lever is inverted and a wing nut is not used (*see* Fig. 70).

in all positions of the adjustable footrests the brake can be conveniently operated without removing the foot from the rest. The adjuster nut (*A*, Fig. 80; *E*, Fig. 70) at the end of the brake rod should be turned *clockwise* to remedy wear. To alter the angle of the brake-pedal lever, proceed thus: loosen the rod adjuster-nut, slacken the brake-pedal stop locknut (*B*, Fig. 80), and adjust the hexagon-headed stop-screw to obtain the best pedal position. Afterwards retighten the lock-nut and adjust the brake rod adjuster-nut as required. Place the gear pedal in neutral and tighten the adjuster-nut until the minimum amount of pedal movement operates the brake without, however, any suspicion of friction when the pedal is released and the wheel is rotated by hand.

Adjustment of the operating mechanism of the front brake is provided on the control-cable adjuster on the forks (girder type) or brake anchor plate (telescopic forks). To adjust on the 1938–9 models, grip the adjuster with a small fixed spanner; then to take up wear of the control cable and friction linings, rotate in an *anti-clockwise* direction after first loosening the lock-nut. After adjustment, retighten this nut. On all later models finger adjustment is provided and the shoes should be made to come as close to the drums as possible without causing friction when the brake is off.

If either brake is harsh in action or tends to squeak, remove the anchor plate (*see* Fig. 79) and file each lining thin for about 1 in. from each end. This slightly reduces the effective area of the brake lining but results in much smoother braking without any appreciable decrease in efficiency. Smooth hard linings should be roughened up with a file, and oily ones cleaned with petrol.

Tyres. Check the tyre inflation pressures (*see* page 4) about once a week and, if found low, pump up to the requisite lb per sq in., using a pressure gauge. Never ride your motor-cycle with the rear tyre deflated, as the fabric of the cover, as well as the tube, suffers severely if this is done, and the damage may be almost irreparable. From time to time inspect the covers with the machine jacked up, and remove all small flints with a sharp penknife. This practice often saves a hold-up on the road, as flints which get embedded in the rubber usually penetrate deeper as the machine is continued to be run.

Never leave the machine standing for a long time unjacked, as this is bad for both wheels and tyres. Also avoid letting the machine stand in a welter of oil or paraffin, which causes tyres to soften and deteriorate very rapidly. Note that "Butyl" tubes retain full pressure much longer than pure rubber tubes.

Sidecar Wheel Alignment. If heavy tyre wear and skidding are to be avoided, it is essential to keep the wheels in proper alignment relative to each other and relative to the frame. The adjuster screws or draw-bolt-adjuster nuts (pre-1956 spring frame) at the chain stays should be adjusted evenly on both sides.

When fitting or refitting a Norton sidecar, place the sidecar in position, leaving all attachment bolts slack. The sidecar wheel should not run parallel with the machine wheels, or there would be a tendency for the machine to constantly pull to the left. The sidecar wheel should toe-in towards the machine $\frac{3}{4}$ in. (*see* Fig. 81).

Alignment is regulated by the clip-lug at the bottom of the sidecar centre arm, and the clip lug of the rear arm. To align correctly, two boards about 6 ft long, 4 in. wide, and 1 in. thick are necessary, which should be placed on the floor, one against the two tyres of the machine, the other against the one tyre of the sidecar. Now measure the distance between the boards immediately in front of the front wheel and at the rear of the rear wheel; the distance between the edges should be $\frac{3}{4}$ in. less at the front than at the rear.

Besides checking the wheels for track, it is desirable to check that the motor-cycle is correctly aligned in a vertical plane. Fig. 82 suggests the best method of verifying this point. Place the outfit on a level floor and then lay a board (about 4 ft long) against the upper part of the front forks on each side of the machine, as indicated. Mark where the board touches the floor and then measure the two dimensions C. It is assumed the board has a straight edge and is rested in the same position on each side of the forks. If the motor-cycle itself is truly vertical, the two dimensions C will, of course, be exactly equal. It is recommended, however, that the motor-

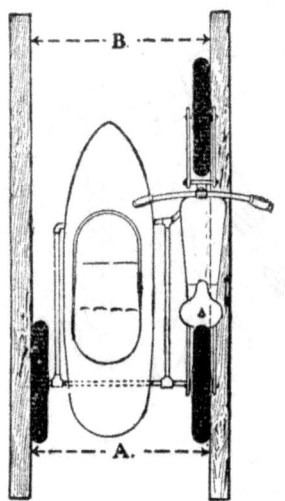

FIG. 81. SIDECAR ALIGNMENT
The distance B should be $\frac{3}{4}$ in. less than the distance A.

cycle itself leans slightly *away* from the sidecar. In this case dimension C on the off-side should be slightly greater than dimension C on the near-side. An excessive outward lean is to be deprecated and is bad for the outfit and its driver. Norton Motors, Ltd., recommend a $\frac{3}{4}$ in. lean over the height of the motor-cycle, measured on a plumb line.

Solo Wheel Alignment. To check the wheel alignment on a solo motor-cycle, use a straight-edged board (about 6 ft long, 1 in. wide, and $\frac{1}{2}$ in. thick), or a taut piece of string. Place the motor-cycle on its stand so that it is quite upright. Then check for correct alignment by holding the straight edge or board in contact with the front and rear tyres. If the wheel alignment is correct, the straight edge or board should contact *each tyre* at the *front and rear*. Rectify faulty alignment by means of the chain adjusters in the rear fork ends (*see* page 115). If dealing with a Model 19R, take into account the fact that the rear wheel has a 4·00–18 rear tyre fitted.

STEERING HEAD, FORKS, FRAME, ETC.

Steering-head Adjustment (1938–46 Girder-forks). See that it allows perfect freedom without up-and-down play. To test this, support the crankcase so that the front wheel clears the ground and slacken the steering damper. Correct adjustment of the head bearings is obtained when the handlebars turn freely without any play.

Play in the steering head is liable to damage the ball races, and also

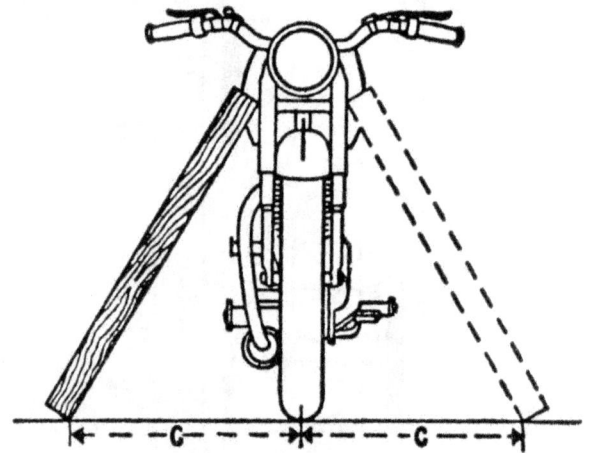

FIG. 82. HOW TO CHECK IF THE MOTOR-CYCLE OF A SIDECAR OUTFIT IS VERTICAL

causes a tendency for instability on grease, as does play in the wheel bearings. To confirm the existence of play, try to lift the front portion of the mudguard and note if movement occurs between the top of the head lug and the bottom of the fork clip. To take up play, slacken the fork clip locking-bolt and tighten the nut above the steering column.

Steering-head Adjustment (Telescopic Forks). Raise the front wheel clear of the ground by placing a suitable box under the engine cradle. Then place the thumb of the left hand on the joint between the steering head and the fork-head clip. Endeavour to lift the front forks with the right hand, when any play in the steering-head races should easily be detected.

If an adjustment is needed, slacken the steering column lock-nut, and also the pinch-bolt which clamps each fork leg to the fork crown. Remove steering-head slackness by adjusting the nut on the steering column below the head clip. Make sure that the telescopic forks are quite free to rotate on the head races and, when the required adjustment has been made, re-tighten the steering column lock-nut and the two pinch-bolts.

Fork-Spindle Adjustment (1938–46). An identical method is used for the two top-spindles and the bottom rear-spindle. First the lock-nuts at each end of each spindle should be slackened. The spindle should then be rotated *anti-clockwise* by means of a spanner applied to its squared end, until the spindle is just tight. Then slacken back about half a turn and tighten up the lock-nuts.

To adjust the bottom front-spindle, first unscrew the shock-absorber knob until the star washer behind is just free. Then slacken the lock-nut and rotate the spindle *clockwise* until just tight. The spindle should then be slackened back about half a turn and the lock-nut re-tightened. Finally check for free fork action.

Shock Absorbers (1938–46). A knob adjuster enables the shock-absorbers to be adjusted to meet all varying road conditions.

Lubrication of Front Forks. Instructions for greasing the fork spindles of girder-type forks (1938–46), and replenishing telescopic-type forks (1947 onwards) with damping oil, are given on page 38.

Removing Telescopic Forks from Frame. The front wheel and mudguard can, if desired, be left in position. First detach the switch panel from the headlamp and remove the steering-damper arm from the frame. Also disconnect the speedometer lighting and driving cables from the speedometer head. Disconnect all control cables from the handlebars and remove the latter.

Completely slacken the steering damper, and remove the steering column lock-nut, complete with damper rod and knob. Next take off the oil filler-plugs and the speedometer panel (pre-1956). Remove the steering-head clip and adjusting nut. Then withdraw the telescopic forks, being careful not to lose any balls from the steering-head races. Also avoid spilling any damping oil from the fork legs. If this happens, subsequent replenishment (*see* page 38) will be necessary.

Fitting Telescopic Forks to Frame. First inspect the steering-head races and balls. There should be 17 balls per race. If the races are pitted, knock them out of their housings and renew. With regard to the races in the frame, each has a small hole provided to permit the entry of grease. See that this is clear. Grease generously the track of the race fitted to the base of the steering column, and the top frame-race. Position the 34 balls and gently insert the steering column through the frame head.

Position the top race and dust cover, and then screw the adjusting nut down the column until the hexagon is bearing lightly against the top race. Now replace the steering-head clip and the speedometer panel. Also fit loosely the steering column locking-nut, and fit and tighten firmly both filler plugs. Afterwards adjust the steering head correctly (*see* page 136), replace the remaining items, and check all nuts and bolts for security.

Dismantling Telescopic Fork Legs. Fig. 83 shows the "innards" of each fork leg, which can be dismantled with the forks fitted to the frame, or removed. A "pull-through" (*see* page 61) may be required to remove and replace the main tube. Dismantle each leg in the following manner—

First remove the front wheel and mudguard. Remove the damping-oil filler, and drain-plugs, from the top and bottom of each fork leg, and drain off the whole of the damping oil. Now slacken the pinch-bolt in the crown lug and proceed to withdraw the fork end, complete with bottom cover, springs, and main tube, To facilitate withdrawing the main tube, screw the "pull-through" into the top end, and tap out with a small mallet.

Remove the top leather washer (which may stick to the inside of the upper cover) from the main tube, also the short buffer-spring (pre-1953) and main spring. Detach the bottom cover, which is held to the fork end by a pair of screws. Take off the leather washer and then remove the locking ring from the top of the fork end. Now draw the fork end off the main tube, and dismantle the few remaining components from the tube.

Assembling Telescopic Forks. Clean carefully all the members comprising each fork leg, and renew worn parts as required. Then secure the bottom bush to the main tube with the retaining nut. Position the fork end on the main tube. Next assemble the shouldered bush into the fork end and fit the vital oil-seal, making quite sure that the radiused side of the leather is at the top. Tighten the locking ring so as to be secure, but such that no distortion of the vital oil-seal case occurs. Replace the smaller of the two leather washers over the locking ring. Then fit the main spring, the buffer spring (pre-1953), and the second leather washer.

Fit the bottom cover and securing screws. Now screw the "pull-through" into the top end of the main tube, and pass through the crown lug and the steering-head clip. With a tommy-bar inserted across the "pull-through," draw the main tube into position. Tighten the pinch-bolt in the crown lug temporarily. Afterwards withdraw the "pull-through," fit the filler plug to the main tube, and loosen the pinch-bolt. Lock the main tube with the filler plug and retighten the pinch-bolt. Finally replace the drain plug, remove the filler plug, and replenish the fork leg with damping oil (*see* page 38).

The Rear Springing. Two types of rear suspension-units have been fitted to Nortons. The 1938–52 units shown in Fig. 84 are of simple

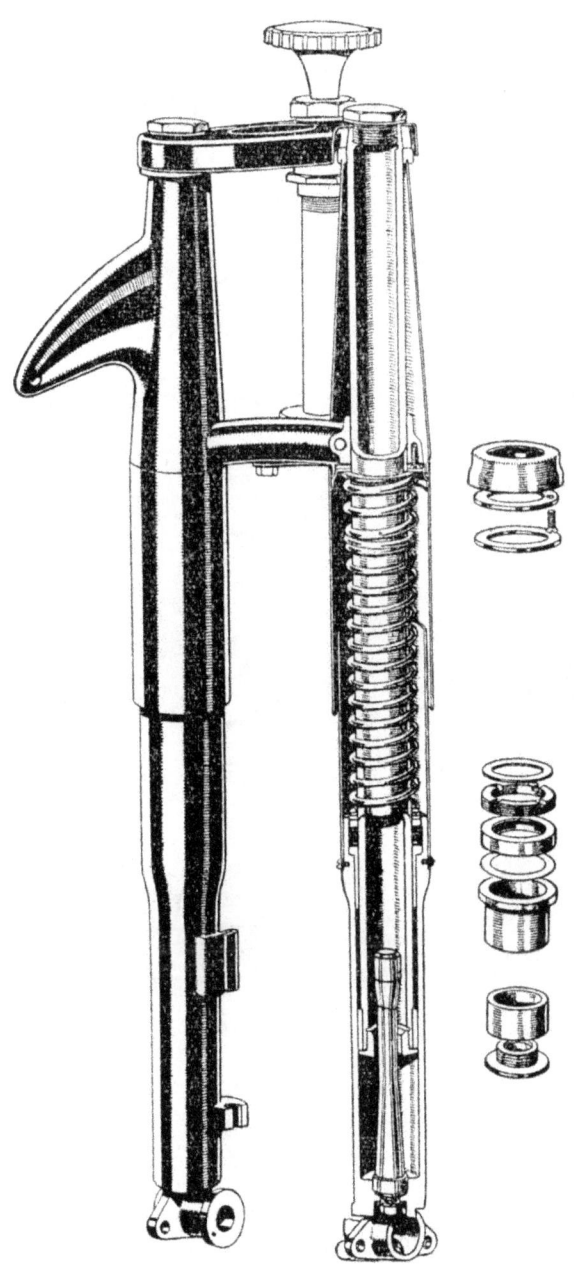

FIG. 83. TELESCOPIC FORKS (1947 ONWARDS)

design and do not embody hydraulic damping. The only maintenance normally required is to keep the units well greased (*see* page 39).

In the case of the "swinging arm" rear suspension-units fitted to 1953 and subsequent spring-frame models, no maintenance whatever is normally needed (*see* page 39) and in the unlikely event of any attention being

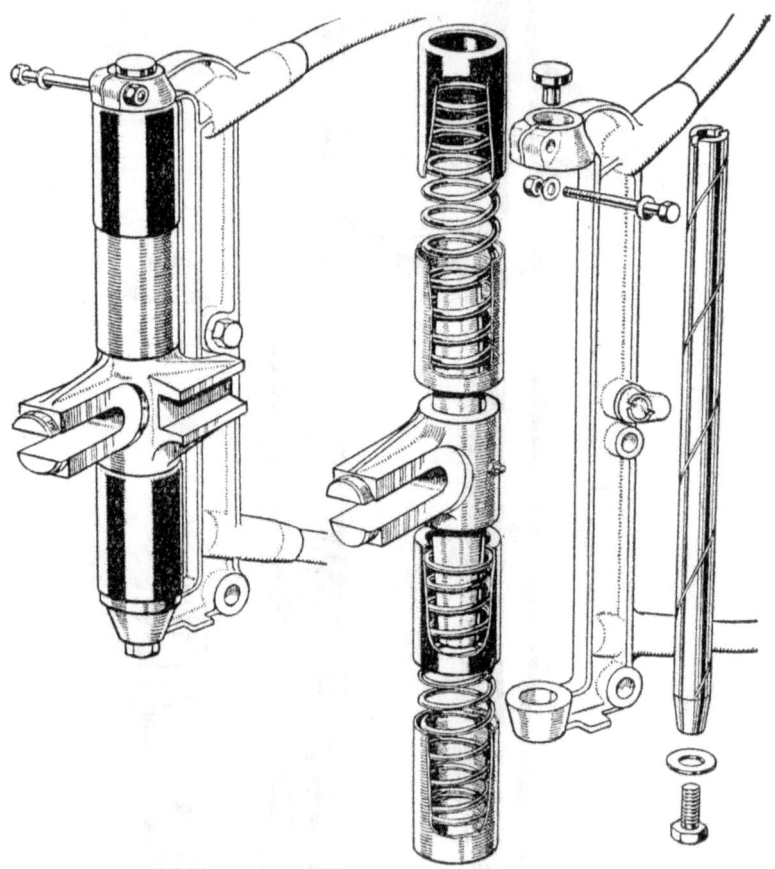

FIG. 84. THE REAR SUSPENSION-UNITS (1938–52)

necessary, the units should be removed and taken to the nearest Norton dealer or distributor. Removal of the units is straightforward. The "swinging arm" pivot requires neither lubrication nor adjustment, but after a big mileage the Silentbloc bushes (*see* page 142) may require to be renewed.

GENERAL MAINTENANCE 141

To Dismantle Rear Suspension-units (1938–52). This should not be necessary until after a very big mileage when some dust may be found to have penetrated past the telescopic covers. To dismantle each unit (Fig. 84) for inspection, cleaning, or spring renewal, proceed as follows—

Remove the rear wheel complete. Next loosen the clip pin across the top of the rear-frame member which secures the stationary-plunger rod. Then unscrew four or five turns the locking pin at the bottom of the rear-frame member, and with a mallet or soft hammer tap out the pin. This frees the stationary plunger from its taper. Now remove completely the bottom locking pin and withdraw upwards the stationary plunger from the frame member.

Insert a tyre lever at the side of the top and bottom covers and between the covers and the frame, as far as possible towards the top of the bottom. A little leverage should now suffice to force the covers away from the frame member and enable the complete assembly to be removed and dealt with. To prevent the springs flying out when removing the assembly, it is a good plan when enough of the central hole is exposed to insert a $\frac{5}{16}$ in. diameter bar threaded at both ends and fitted with large wing nuts.

To Reassemble (1938–52). After inspecting and cleaning the various parts, smear a little oil on the fork-end bearing surface and replace the springs and covers in position on the fork end. See that the stronger spring is refitted at the top. Now reinsert the assembly into the jaw of the rear-frame member. This may be rather difficult unless the springs are first compressed to occupy a space slightly less than that of the rear-frame member. To overcome the difficulty, use the bar referred to above for dismantling. After positioning the spring assembly into the rear-member jaw, remove the bar and fit the assembly into its approximate position. Smear the stationary plunger with oil, insert the taper end first into the upper hole in the rear member. It should not be difficult to push the plunger home because the tapered end readily draws the cups into correct alignment. Finally replace the bottom locking-pin and tighten the top clip-pin.

Be careful when replacing the rear wheel to see that the fork ends are as nearly parallel with each other as possible and that the open end of the jaw faces to the rear. Also when adjusting the secondary chain (*see* page 115) avoid letting the rear wheel be moved farther along the fork end away from the plunger than is absolutely necessary, otherwise the wheel spindle may be unduly stressed. If a big chain adjustment is necessary, remove a link from the chain.

Removing and Dismantling "Swinging Arm" (1953 Onwards). Should dismantling become necessary after a big mileage in order to renew the Silentbloc bushes, do this in the following manner. First remove the rear wheel, as described on page 128. Next take off the rear suspension-units after removing the bolts which secure the top and bottom members to the frame and "swinging arm" respectively (*see* Fig. 85). Remove the outer portion of the oil-bath chain-case (*see* page 117) and also the clutch (*see* page 118); remove the nut from the off-side of the pivot bolt. Then drift out the pivot bolt and withdraw the "swinging arm."

To Remove Silentbloc Bushes. To remove the bushes from the "swinging arm," knock them out with a suitable drift. This should have a diameter

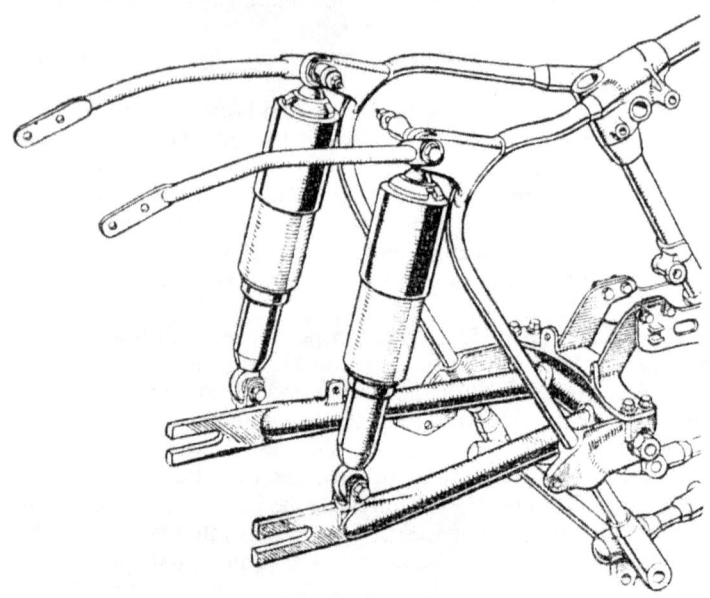

FIG. 85. THE "SWINGING ARM" REAR SUSPENSION
(1953 ONWARDS)
(*By courtesy of "The Motor Cycle," London*)

only slightly smaller than the inside diameter of the cross tube. Its length must be greater than the hole in the Silentbloc outer-sleeve. If difficulty is experienced in removing the bushes, soak them in suitable oil.

To Assemble and Replace "Swinging Arm" (**1953 Onwards**). Drift or press one new Silentbloc bush into the "swinging arm" until its outer sleeve is level with the extremity of the cross tube. From the opposite side insert the distance-piece and drift or press right home the second Silentbloc bush. Then position the "swinging arm," being careful to see that the brackets for attaching the suspension units are on the top side (*see* Fig. 85). Finally replace the pivot bolt, fit the nut to the off-side, and securely tighten it.

INDEX

ACCESSORY firms, 58
Advance, ignition, 98
Air lever, 3, 103
Aligning headlamp, 22
Alignment, wheel, 134–6
Amal carburettor, 40–57
Ammeter, 15

BATTERY—
  connexions, 18
  filler, 17
  topping-up, 15
Big-end bearing, 32, 111
Brake—
  adjustment, 133
  dismantling, 131
  lubrication, 39
Brushes, dynamo, 12
Bulb renewal, 25–6
"Butyl" tubes, 134

CARBON, removing, 79, 92
Carburettor—
  assembling, 56–7
  details, 40–6
  dismantling, 52–5
  settings, 48, 50
  tuning, 47–52
Chain—
  case, removing, 117
  lubrication, 36–8
  stretch, 116
  whip, 114–15
Chromium, cleaning, 62
Circlips—
  brake pivot-pin, 132
  clutch, 118, 121
  gudgeon-pin, 91
Cleaning—
  carburettor, 55
  chromium, 62
  contacts, 68
  enamel, 62
  engine, 62

Cleaning (*contd.*)—
  gearbox, 62
  lamps, 24
  sparking plug, 64
Clutch—
  adjustment, 113–14
  dismantling, 116, 118
  springs, 121
  wear, 120
Colloidal graphite, 4
Commutator, 13
Compensated voltage control, 14
Connecting-rod bearings, 111
Contact-breaker gap, 66
Controls—
  adjusting, 1
  setting for starting, 5
  use of, 2
Crankcase—
  bearings, 112
  draining, 35
  splitting, 112
Cut-away, throttle, 44, 51
C.V.C. unit, 14
Cylinder barrel, removing, 75–7, 86, 90

DECARBONIZING, 73–96
Degree disc, 98
Draining—
  crankcase, 35
  oil tank, 34
Dry-sump lubrication system, 30–3
Dynamo maintenance, 11–15

EASY starter, 43
Electrolyte level, 16
Enamel, cleaning, 62
Engine—
  installing, 113
  number, 58
  oils, 33
  overhaul, 102–13
  pinion key-ways, 99
  removing, 110

Exhaust—
  flame, 47
  valve lifter, 3, 72, 103

FILTER, oil tank, 34
Flange, carburettor, 56
Float chamber, 55
Flywheel assembly, 111–12
Focusing headlamp, 23
Foot gear-change, dismantling, 121–3
Fork-spindle adjustment, 137
Frame number, 58
Front—
  brake adjustment, 133
  forks, removing, 137
  wheel, removing, 126–7
Fuel—
  consumption, high, 52
  replenishment, 4
Fuses, 15

GAP—
  contact-breaker, 66
  sparking plug, 63
Gear—
  change, dismantling, 121–3
  changing, 7
Gearbox—
  cover, removing, 121
  exploded views, 122, 124
  lubrication, 35
  overhaul, 125
  removing, 125
Greases, suitable, 38
Grinding-in—
  cylinder head, 82
  valves, 81
Gudgeon-pin—
  fit, 112
  removal, 91

HEADLAMPS, 18–22
Horn, 26
H.T. cable, removing, 69
Hub—
  bearings, 126
  dismantling, 129–31
  lubrication, 39
Hydrometer readings, 17

IGNITION—
  lever, 3, 103
  timing, 96–8

Inflation pressures, 4
Inserts, clutch, 120

JET—
  block, 56
  needle, 44, 51

LUBRICATION—
  brakes, 39
  chart, 37
  control levers, 39
  engine, 30–5
  front forks, 38
  gearbox, 36
  "Magdyno," 35
    chain, 33
  primary chain, 36
  rear springing, 39
  rocker-box, 35
  secondary chain, 38
  speedometer-drive gearbox, 39
  steering head, 38
  wheel hubs, 39

"MAGDYNO"—
  contact-breaker, 66–8
  lubrication, 35
  removing, 102
  timing, 96
Main jet, 44, 49
Maintenance, items for, 58
"Monobloc" carburettor, 45

NEEDLE-JET, 44
Neutral, obtaining, 8
Nipple, soldering, 105
Nuts, checking for tightness, 63

OIL—
  bath, removing, 117
    cover, removing, 116
  circulation, 7, 33
  control ring, 91, 93
  pressure control-valve, 31, 34, 106
  pump, 30
    dismantling, 106
  replenishment, 4
  tank, draining, 34

PETROL tank, removing, 73
Pick-up, h.t., 68

INDEX

Pilot—
   air screw, 44, 50
   jet, 50, 52
Piston—
   removal, 91
   rings, 78, 82, 92
   seizure, 9
Pitted contacts, 67
Pressure gauges, 4
Primary chain—
   adjustment, 114
   lubrication, 36

REAR—
   brake adjustment, 133
   springing, 39, 139–42
   wheel, removing, 126–9
Rebore, 92
Restriction jet, 101
Riding position, 1
Rocker—
   box, dismantling, 108–9
     lubrication, 33, 35
   bushes, 109
Running-in, 9

SECONDARY chain—
   adjustment, 115
   lubrication, 38
Seizure, piston, 9
Shims, rocker, 109
Shock-absorber—
   clutch, 116, 119
   fork, 137
Sidecar—
   lamps, 23
   wheel alignment, 134
   removal, 127
Silentbloc bushes, removing, 142
Slip-ring, 68
Slow-running, bad, 52
Small-end bearing, 111–12
Solo wheel alignment, 135
Spares, ordering, 58
Sparking plug—
   cleaning, 64
   gap, 63
   types recommended, 9
Specific gravity, checking, 17
Spring link, 116
Starting engine, 6

Steering head—
   adjustment, 136
   lubrication, 38
Stop-tail lamp, 24, 26
Storing battery, 18
Suspension units, rear, 139–42
"Swinging arm," removing, 141
Switch, lighting, 22, 26

TAPPETS, replacing, 107
"Tekall," 62
Telescopic forks, 38, 137
Terminals, dynamo, 13
Throttle—
   needle clip, 55
   stop, 43
   valve, 55
Timing—
   cover, 101, 106–8
   gear bushes, 108
   gears, removing, 104, 106
   "Magdyno," 96–8
   valve, 98–100
Toe-in, sidecar, 134
Tool kit, 60
Tools, proprietary, 61
Top-dead-centre, finding, 96
Topping-up battery, 15
Transmission, 113–26
Tuning carburettor, 47–52
Twist-grip throttle, 2, 103
Tyre—
   maintenance, 134
   pressures, 4

UNMARKED timing gears, 99
Upper-cylinder lubricants, 4

VALVE—
   clearances, 69–72
   guides, 110
   removal, 80–1, 91
   timing, 98–100
Vents, battery, 15

WHEEL—
   alignment, 134–6
   bearings, 126
   hubs, dismantling, 129–31
   removal, 126–9
Wiring diagrams, 27–9

OTHER MOTORCYCLE MANUALS AVAILABLE IN THIS SERIES

AJS (BOOK OF) ALL MODELS 1955-1965:
350cc & 500cc Singles ~ Models 16, 16S, 18, 18S

ARIEL WORKSHOP MANUAL 1933-1951:
All single, twin & 4 cylinder models

ARIEL (BOOK OF) MAINTENANCE & REPAIR MANUAL 1932-1939:
LF3, LF4, LG, NF3, NF4, NG, OG, VA, VA3, VA4, VB, VF3, VF4, VG, Red Hunter LH, NH, OH, VH & Square Four 4F, 4G, 4H

BMW FACTORY WORKSHOP MANUAL R27, R28:
English, German, French and Spanish text

BMW FACTORY WORKSHOP MANUAL R50, R50S, R60, R69S:
Also includes a supplement for the USA models: R50US, R60US, R69US.
English, German, French and Spanish text

BSA PRE-WAR SINGLES & TWINS (BOOK OF) 1936-1939:
All Pre-War single & twin cylinder SV & OHV models through 1939
150cc, 250cc, 350cc, 500cc, 600cc, 750cc & 1,000cc

BSA SINGLES (BOOK OF) 1945-1954:
OHV & SV 250cc, 350cc, 500cc & 600cc, Groups B, C & M

BSA SINGLES (BOOK OF) 1955-1967:
B31, B32, B33, B34 and "Star" B40 & SS90

BSA 250cc SINGLES (BOOK OF) 1954-1970:
B31, B32, B33, B34 and "Star" B40 & SS90

BSA TWINS (BOOK OF) 1948-1962:
All 650cc & 500cc twins

BSA TWINS (SECOND BOOK OF) 1962-1969:
All 650cc & 500cc, A50 & A65 OHV unit construction twins

DUCATI OHC FACTORY WORKSHOP MANUAL:
160 Junior Monza, 250 Monza, 250 GT, 250 Mark 3, 250 Mach 1, 250 SCR & 350 Sebring

HONDA 250 & 305cc FACTORY WORKSHOP MANUAL:
C.72 C.77 CS.72, CS.77, CB.72, CB.77 [HAWK]

HONDA 125 & 150cc FACTORY WORKSHOP MANUAL:
C.92, CS.92, CB.92, C.95 & CA.95

HONDA 90 (BOOK OF) ALL MODELS UP TO 1966:
All 90cc variations including the S90, CM90, C200, S65, Trail 90 & C65 models

HONDA 50cc FACTORY WORKSHOP MANUAL: C.100

HONDA 50cc FACTORY WORKSHOP MANUAL: C.110

HONDA (BOOK OF) MAINTENANCE & REPAIR 1960-1966:
50cc C.100, C.102, C.110 & C.114 ~ 125cc C.92 & CB.92
250cc C.72 & CB.72 ~ 305cc CB.77

LAMBRETTA (BOOK OF) MAINTENANCE & REPAIR:
125 & 150cc, all models up to 1958, except model "48".

LAMBRETTA (SECOND BOOK OF) MAINTENANCE & REPAIR:
125, 150, 175 & 200cc, all Li & TV models and derivates from 1958 to 1970.

MATCHLESS SINGLES (BOOK OF) 1945-1956:
350 & 500cc OHV Touring Singles G3L, G80, G3LS & G80S

MATCHLESS SINGLES (BOOK OF) 1955-1966:
350 & 500cc OHV Touring Singles G3LS, G3S, G3, G80S, G80, Mercury, Mercury Sports, Major & Major Sports

NORTON DOMINATOR TWINS (BOOK OF) 1955-1965
500, 600 & 650cc Dominator Twins and 750cc Atlas

NORTON FACTORY TWIN CYLINDER WORKSHOP MANUAL: 1957-1970: *Lightweight Twins:* 250cc Jubilee, 350cc Navigator and 400cc Electra and the *Heavyweight Twins:* Model 77, 88, 88SS, 99, 99SS, Sports Special, Manxman, Mercury, Atlas, G15, P11, N15, Ranger (P11A).

NORTON (BOOK OF) MAINTENANCE & REPAIR 1932-1939:
All Pre-War SV, OHV and OHC models: 16H, 16I, 18, 19, 20, 50, 55, ES2, CJ, CSI, International 30 & 40

SUZUKI 200 & 250cc FACTORY WORKSHOP MANUAL:
250cc T20 [X-6 Hustler] ~ 200cc T200 [X-5 Invader & Sting Ray Scrambler]

SUZUKI 250cc FACTORY WORKSHOP MANUAL: 250cc ~ T10

TRIUMPH (BOOK OF) MAINTENANCE & REPAIR 1935-1939:
All Pre-War single & twin cylinder models: L2/1, 2/1, 2/5, 3/1, 3/2, 3/5, 5/1, 5/2, 5/3, 5/4, 5/5, 5/10, 6/1, Tiger 70, 80, 90 & 2H. Tiger 70C, 3S & 3H, Tiger 80C & 5H, Tiger 90C, 6S, 2HC & 3SC, 5T & 5S and T100

TRIUMPH 1937-1951 WORKSHOP MANUAL (A. St. J. Masters):
Covers rigid frame and sprung hub single cylinder SV & OHV and twin cylinder OHV pre-war, military, and post-war models

TRIUMPH 1945-1955 FACTORY WORKSHOP MANUAL NO.11:
Covers pre-unit, twin-cylinder rigid frame, sprung hub, swing-arm and 350cc, 500cc & 650cc.

VELOCETTE (BOOK OF) MAINTENANCE & REPAIR:
Covers LE Mk. I, II, & III, Valiant, Vogue, MOV, MAC, KSS, KTS, Viper, Venom & Thruxton. Includes some limited material on the Viceory scooter

VESPA (BOOK OF) MAINTENANCE & REPAIR 1946-1959:
All 125cc & 150cc models including 42/L2 & Gran Sport

VINCENT WORKSHOP MANUAL 1935-1955:
All Series A, B & C Models

COMING SOON IN THIS SAME SERIES:

BRIDGESTONE FACTORY WORKSHOP MANUAL: 50 Sport, 60 Sport,
90 De Luxe, 90 Trail, 90 Mountain, 90 Sport, 175 Dual Twin & Hurricane

BRITISH MILITARY MAINTENANCE & REPAIR MANUAL:
Service & Repair data for all British WD motorcycles

BRITISH MOTORCYCLE ENGINES: By the staff of "The Motor Cycle"

CEZETTA 175cc MODEL 501 SCOOTER MANUAL & PARTS BOOK

VILLIERS ENGINE WORKSHOP MANUAL: All Villiers engines through 1947

BSA BANTAM (BOOK OF) 1948-1970:
D7, D7D/L, D10, D14/4 & Bantam 175

HONDA 50 (BOOK OF):
C100, C102, C110, C114, P50, PC50, PF50, C50 (Also applicable to C100 Series Monkey Bike and CE105H Trail Bike

Please check our website at
www.VelocePress.com
For our most up-to-date listing

www.ingramcontent.com/pod-product-compliance
Lightning Source LLC
Chambersburg PA
CBHW070551170426
43201CB00012B/1808